TEILHARD DE CHARDIN:
AN ANALYSIS AND ASSESSMENT

TEILHARD DE CHARDIN

An analysis and assessment

D. GARETH JONES

William B. Eerdmans Publishing Company
Grand Rapids, Michigan

*This edition published by special arrangement with
Inter-Varsity Press, Downers Grove, Illinois 60515.*

*Inter-Varsity Press
is the book publishing division of
Inter-Varsity Christian Fellowship.*

*SBN 0-87784-540-9
Library of Congress Catalog Card Number: 70-127933*

Printed in the United States of America

CONTENTS

Preface   7

Introduction   11

1 TEILHARD'S LIFE AND THOUGHT   15
   Teilhard's life—The essential components of his thought

2 THE PROJECT   28
   A phenomenology of the universe—The nature of his science—The
   law of complexity-consciousness—The future—Christology—Further
   aspects of his theology—Dialogue with Marxists

3 AN APPRAISAL   64
   The way forward

PREFACE

Since the publication of the English translation of *The Phenomenon of Man*[1] in 1959, a considerable number of Teilhard de Chardin's works have appeared in this country. These range from devotional works, such as *Le Milieu Divin*,[2] *The Mass on the World*[3] and *Christ in the World of Matter*,[3] to a collection of palaeontological writings, *The Appearance of Man*,[4] to collections of his letters, for example *Letters from a Traveller*[5] and *The Making of a Mind*,[6] and to largely speculative writings, for instance *The Future of Man*.[7] *The Vision of the Past*[8] and *Writings in Time of War*[9] are partly speculative and partly scientific in the first case, and partly speculative and partly devotional in the second.

Alongside the appearance of these books, many analyses of the man as a person, as a scientist and as a thinker have also been produced. Foremost among these are the studies by Claude Cuénot,[10] Emile Rideau,[11] Christopher F. Mooney,[12] N. M. Wildiers,[13] Henri de Lubac[14] and Helmut de Terra.[15]

[1] Collins. Abbreviated to *PM* in references. Page numbers refer Fontana edition (1965).
[2] Collins, 1960. Page numbers refer to Fontana edition (1964).
[3] Published as parts of *Hymn of the Universe* (Collins, 1965).
[4] Collins, 1965.   [5] Collins, 1962.   [6] Collins, 1965.
[7] Collins, 1964.   [8] Collins, 1966.   [9] Collins, 1968.
[10] *Teilhard de Chardin* (Burns and Oates, 1965).
[11] *Teilhard de Chardin : A Guide to his Thought* (Collins, 1967).
[12] *Teilhard de Chardin and the Mystery of Christ* (Collins, 1966).
[13] *An Introduction to Teilhard de Chardin* (Collins, Fontana, 1968).
[14] *The Religion of Teilhard de Chardin* (Collins, 1967). Also, a much briefer work, *Teilhard Explained* (Paulist Press, 1968).
[15] *Memories of Teilhard de Chardin* (Collins, 1964).

With the profusion of books and pamphlets on Teilhard, it may be expected that, taken together, they would represent a wide variety of opinion on the merits or otherwise of Teilhard's synthesis. This, however, is not the case. The majority of writers are committed, either wholly or in large part, to Teilhard's phenomenology. Furthermore, most of them are also Roman Catholics, a notable exception being C. E. Raven, who contributed to our knowledge of Teilhard's thought with *Teilhard de Chardin: Scientist and Seer*.[16] More fundamentally, whether Roman Catholics or not, they are characterized by their radical religious views, and it is these views which allow them to espouse so fully Teilhard's approach to God, Christ and the world.

Although some of the works already mentioned do contain critical sections, these are usually submerged beneath a general bias towards his world-view. Books, pamphlets and articles directed against Teilhard or showing concern about many of his basic beliefs can be found,[17] but they are mostly not readily obtainable by the lay public. The result of this is that Teilhard's views have become known chiefly through the works of those eager to forward his cause. The lack of public discussion with those who are sceptical about certain of his claims has led to a glaringly biased presentation of his views. The reaction of the public has been correspondingly extreme; either acceptance of Teilhard as a prophet and almost infallible leader or rejection of his massive speculations as nonsense.

[16] Collins, 1962.

[17] Of those available in English, we may cite: P. B. Medawar, 'Critical note' in *Mind, 70* (1961), pp. 99-106; G. G. Simpson, 'On the remarkable testament of the Jesuit paleontologist Pierre Teilhard de Chardin' in *Scientific American, 202* (1960), pp. 201-207; Olivier Rabut, *Dialogue with Teilhard de Chardin* (Sheed and Ward, 1961); H. Blocher, 'Teilhard de Chardin's cosmic vision: a French Protestant view' in *Interchange, 1* (1967), pp. 9-20; H. Blocher, 'The mystic vision of Teilhard de Chardin: a French Protestant view' in *Interchange, 1* (1967), pp. 71-82; R. Hooykaas, 'Teilhardism, a pseudo-scientific delusion' in *Free University Quarterly, 9* (1963), pp. 1-57; R. Hooykaas, 'Teilhardism, its predecessors, adherents and critics' in *Free University Quarterly, 9* (1963), pp. 58-83; Cornelius Van Til, 'Pierre Teilhard de Chardin' in *The Westminster Theological Journal, 28* (1966), pp. 109-144.

The situation has been worsened by the aggressive attitude adopted by some of Teilhard's followers to criticisms of his writings. Even mild criticism tends to be met, in some instances, by heated rebuffs rather than by open discussion. The characterization of Teilhard as 'Teilhard crucified',[18] simply because his ideas are criticized in some quarters, is an example of such sensitive over-reaction.

The present little book is an attempt to look at Teilhard through the eyes of one who is not initially committed to his presuppositions and his ways of thinking. But neither is it an attempt to debunk him or an excuse for pouring scorn on his search for unity in the contemporary world. It is written with the aim of trying to discover what this attractive and enigmatic man has to say to a world shattered for want of a satisfying hope and compelling purpose in existence. It is written, moreover, from the standpoint of a committed Christian and a working biologist; one who believes he has found ultimate meaning for his own life in the person of Jesus Christ as his Saviour and Lord, and one who finds excitement and hope in scientific endeavour.

Starting from these basic principles there is ample room for formulating a comprehensive world-view. With this in mind, and recognizing the need for such an over-all system as a guide to the contemporary scientific world, Teilhard's contribution to this problem cannot be ignored. His far-ranging ideas must be faced; his underlying presuppositions must be analysed. It is in this spirit that the following pages have been written.

It is also important to study Teilhard for other reasons. Frequently, in symposia[19] and individual studies[20] on the relationship between science and religious faith, the views of Teilhard as alluded to, while the scientifico-humanist aspects of his writings were thought worthy of consideration by a number of the contributors to *The Humanist Frame*.[21] He

[18] A chapter heading in Paul Chauchard's book *Teilhard de Chardin on Love and Suffering* (Paulist Press, 1966).

[19] Ian Ramsey (editor), *Biology and Personality* (Blackwell, 1965).

[20] Alistair Hardy, *The Living Stream* (Collins, 1965); W. H. Thorpe, *Science, Man and Morals* (Methuen, 1965).

[21] Edited by J. Huxley (Allen and Unwin, 1961).

cannot be ignored, then, if only by reason of his widespread influence in certain scientific, humanistic and religious circles.

Finally, there is the question of his importance within the sphere of Roman Catholic thinking. The change in the attitude of his church towards him has been remarkable. Whereas his works were banned by the church up until his death in 1955, a far more liberal attitude towards his writings has been evident in the last few years. He is referred to with adulation by many of the progressives within the Roman Catholic church, and one gets the impression that it is his influence which is the spearhead of much of the New Catholicism. He has been described by one writer[22] as the ' prophet ' of the New Catholicism, for the reason that the emphasis on relativism in their ' new theology ' can probably be traced, in large part, to his influence.

Some of the material in this book appeared originally in the form of an article in *Faith and Thought* (the journal of the Victoria Institute), and as a review article in *The Christian Graduate*. I would like to thank the committees of the London and Oxford Christian Graduates' Societies for the opportunities they afforded me to deliver papers on Teilhard, and hence to develop my ideas on this subject. Perhaps most of all I would like to express my thanks to those who have repeatedly encouraged me to continue with this work. Apart from them I would have transferred my allegiance long ago to one or more of the many other scientific and religious topics which interest me so greatly.

D. GARETH JONES

[22] W. Hurvey Woodson, ' The new Roman Catholicism ' in *The Banner of Truth*, no. 58-59 (1968), p. 41.

INTRODUCTION

For many people the world is meaningless and absurd. Being unable to find any purpose in life, they are filled with despair. Realizing that human activity has been robbed of all hope and nobility, their anguish is complete. The world in which they live is vast and impersonal, remote and pointless, while man himself is an irrelevant bauble stumbling along pathetically and tragically into an irrelevant future. Why should man strive to improve himself, when he feels lost and utterly insignificant in the spatial and temporal vastness of an evolving world? Why should man attempt to secure and prolong his future, when his only ultimate hope is cosmic death? What is man's relationship to God, if there is no God? Where is man going, if he is going nowhere? What reliance can man place upon the world, if one day the world will discard him? What can man think of himself, if he is capable of destroying himself?

Modern man is dominated by an existential fear of himself, of his own powers and of the world around him. Lacking any absolutes and certainties in life, he has abandoned himself to despair and has relinquished his responsibility to fulfil himself. Man's great adventure is in danger of grinding to a halt for lack of a stimulus to purposeful and creative living, which in turn is dependent upon a dynamic relationship to God and the world.

For Teilhard, it is this anxiety in the face of the apparent futility of human life which constitutes one of the essential experiences underlying his cosmic synthesis. Teilhard was one with modern man in experiencing the world's hostility, a

fact that appears repeatedly in his writings. In *Le Milieu
Divin,* for example, he could write: ' . . . on certain days the
world seems a terrifying thing: huge, blind and brutal. It
buffets us about, drags us along, kills us with complete indiffer-
ence, . . . sweeps away in one moment what we had laboriously
built up and beautified with all our intelligence and all our
love.'[1] In similar vein he writes in *The Phenomenon of Man* :
' The whole psychology of modern disquiet is linked with the
sudden confrontation with space-time. . . . Conscious or not,
anguish — a fundamental anguish of being — despite our
smiles, strikes in the depths of our hearts and is the undertone
of all our conversations. . . . In the first and most widespread
degree, the " malady of space-time " manifests itself as a rule
by a feeling of futility, of being crushed by the enormities of
the cosmos. . . . Sickness of the dead end — the anguish of
feeling shut in.'[2] A year before he died, he could still echo
the same sentiment: ' Fear of being lost in a world so vast . . .
that man seems to have lost all significance. Fear of being
reduced to immobility. Fear of being unable to find a
way out.'[3]

What emerges from these quotations is the need Teilhard
felt, both for himself and for mankind as a whole, to find a
' way out ',[4] a purpose for man. Apart from such a ' way out ',
thought, the fruit of millions of years of effort, is stifled, still-
born in a self-abortive and absurd universe.[5] What is more,
it is only a ' way out ' which can impart to mankind the ' taste
for life ' and the impetus to continue with its work and to
build the future.

Success or failure, advance or stagnation, life or death.
These were the fundamental dialectics of Teilhard's life, and
they formed the fundamental anxiety of his life. A ' way out '
had to be found, if man was to flourish and develop on the
earth. There must be a successful outcome for man's earthly
achievement. ' I believe this through inference. . . . I believe
this through personal need. . . . Most of all perhaps, I believe
this through love, for I love the world around me too much
not to have confidence in it '.[6]

[1] Pp. 128, 129.   [2] Pp. 249-252.
[3] Quoted by C. F. Mooney, *Teilhard de Chardin and the Mystery
of Christ,* p. 17.   [4] *Idem.*   [5] *PM,* p. 256.   [6] Mooney, *op. cit.,* p. 20.

It is clear that, whatever the form of Teilhard's eventual synthesis, it would be a reflection of a deeply-felt psychological need. Because of the strong currents responsible for its formulation, it would be a personal and an existential synthesis, as opposed to a purely intellectual one. Its success would depend upon the extent to which it provided man with a purposeful existence, in terms of man's latent powers to develop the earth.

From here it is but a short step to the second factor of importance for an understanding of Teilhard's view of the world. By temperament and occupation he knew himself to be ' a child of earth ', whereas by upbringing and intellectual training he felt himself to be ' a child of heaven '.[7] Consequently, the dilemma confronting him was how he could reconcile love for God and love of the world. As he wrote at the beginning of his scientific career: ' a reconciliation must be possible between cosmic love of the world and heavenly love of God . . . between the cult of progress and the passion for the glory of God.'[8] He was not content only to reconcile the two, however; his aim was to incorporate them into a coherent, living unity, which would form the basis for a course of action orientated at one and the same time on both God and the world. In his own words: ' Somewhere there must be a standpoint from which Christ and the earth can be so situated in relation to one another that it is impossible for me to possess the one without embracing the other, to be in communion with the one without being absorbed into the other, to be absolutely Christian without being desperately human.'[9]

The problem confronting Teilhard was how he could be both truly Christian and fully a man, faithful to the thinking of his own day and faithful to the gospel. As Rideau phrased it: ' is it possible to hold the crucified God before ones eyes, while still being passionately devoted to human enterprise and the full development of man? Can one love the world and God? Is secular history inseparable from sacred history?'[10]

The relation between God and the universe is central to Teilhard's thinking, and as with the problem of his anxiety

7 N. M. Wildiers, *An Introduction to Teilhard de Chardin*, p. 22.
8 Quoted by Wildiers, *ibid.*, p. 25.   9 *Idem.*
10 E. Rideau, *Teilhard de Chardin : A Guide to his Thought*, p. 10.

over the outcome of man's worldly endeavours, it is an existential question. It was as though his existence as a human
being and as a Christian were at stake. Consequently, his
solution is more the outcome of a personal encounter with
life, and so of a subjective experience, than of a purely scientific enquiry.[11] It is not surprising, therefore, to learn that Teilhard envisaged the whole adventure of his inner life as being
the Christification of matter.

Both these fundamental problems — his anxiety over finding a 'way out', and his love for God and the world — were
solved by Teilhard in the same general way. By constructing
a vast synthesis incorporating the whole of reality, and based
upon an all-embracing evolutionism and an all-penetrating
Christianity, both problems were accommodated. By placing
man at the summit of the evolutionary process and by insist-
ing that the cosmos is held together by spirit and not matter,
and that it converges towards persons and not things,[12] Teilhard was able to confer upon evolution a direction, a goal and
hence meaning and purpose. By bringing together a religion
of the Christic type and an evolution of the convergent type,
he could view as one his Christianity and his science, as ultimately — at Omega — the spiritual process and the natural
process would coincide.

He was thus able to hold together what he described as ' cosmic sense ' and ' Christic sense '. By cosmic sense, he meant
the cosmic affinity binding us psychologically with the All,
while for him Christic sense meant the conviction on the part
of Christians that Christ constitutes the centre and the final
goal of all things.[13] In bringing together these two concepts,
he gave to Christ a cosmic function, centring everything in the
universe upon a Point, upon a Person, that is Jesus. The point
of contact between the cosmic sense and the Christic sense is
to be found in the certainty that there exists a ' way out ', a
certainty which he derived from his Christian faith.[14]

[11] Wildiers, *op. cit.*, p. 26.   [12] Mooney, *op. cit.*, p. 22.
[13] Wildiers, *op. cit.*, p. 22.   [14] Mooney, *op. cit.*, p. 25.

1 TEILHARD'S LIFE AND THOUGHT

' Teilhard de Chardin was a great evolutionary thinker, comparable with Marx and Darwin; he was at the same time a mystic with a vision as great as St. Augustine's.'[1]

' The greater part of (*The Phenomenon of Man*) . . . is nonsense, tricked out by a variety of tedious metaphysical conceits, and its author can be excused of dishonesty only on the grounds that before deceiving others he has taken great pains to deceive himself.'[2]

The world of Teilhard de Chardin, like the world of his admirers and critics, is characterized by extremes. A priest of the Roman Catholic church, but accepted far more warmly by evolutionary humanists, he has been variously described as a ' genius ',[3] an ' apostle of evolution ',[4] a ' mystic visionary '.[5] The influence of his writings since his death in 1955 has been enormous, so much so that one writer was led to remark that in some quarters they were treated as though inspired writ.[6]

His critics, with just as little restraint, have described *The Phenomenon of Man* as anything from ' a hodgepodge of semi-materialistic, naturalistic speculations ',[7] to ' tipsy, euphoric

[1] From a leaflet issued by ' The Pierre Teilhard de Chardin Association of Great Britain and Ireland '.
[2] P. B. Medawar, *Mind*, 70 (1961), p. 99.
[3] *The Times Literary Supplement*, 25 May 1962, p. 366.
[4] C. Cuénot, *Teilhard de Chardin*, p. 383.
[5] W. H. Thorpe, *Science, Man and Morals*, p. 56.
[6] *The Times Literary Supplement*, op. cit., p. 365.
[7] R. Hooykaas, *Free University Quarterly*, 9 (1963), p. 55.

prose-poetry '.[8]

As for the man himself, he evoked universal warmth and affection, even in those who disagreed with his views. And so one critic has described him as ' a great soul, a kindly man and a subtle mystic '.[9] To one admirer his personal quality was so precious that he could only describe it as ' a state of pre-beatitude '.[10]

Teilhard's self-description is revealing: ' I am a pilgrim of the future on the way back from a journey made entirely in the past.'[11] With his craving after the imperishable and with his desire to see all the elements of the world synthesized in Christ, his spiritual mission was to give back to Christians a true sense of the earth and so he devoted himself to ' manifest and exalt the divino-Christic power contained in the unitary development of the tangible world '.[12] In the light of this it does not surprise us to learn that he considered it the priest's duty to ' Christify ' evolution.[13]

TEILHARD'S LIFE

Born in 1881 in Auvergne, he was the fourth of eleven children in a devout Roman Catholic family. At the age of ten he went to a Jesuit college where he became very interested in geology and mineralogy. At eighteen he entered the Society of Jesus. During the early part of his training with the Society, the community was expelled from France and went to Jersey. On completing this part of his studies in 1905, he was sent for three years to Cairo where he taught chemistry and physics, after which he came to England to complete his studies for the priesthood. It was during his stay in England that his view of the world began to expand.

During the First World War he served as a stretcher-bearer, distinguishing himself by his fortitude and courage. The importance of this period for his world-view lay in the develop-

[8] Medawar, op. cit., p. 99.
[9] G. G. Simpson, Scientific American, 202 (1960), p. 207.
[10] Cuénot, op. cit., p. 382.
[11] Quoted by N. Braybrooke (editor), Teilhard de Chardin : Pilgrim of the Future (Libra Books, 1966), p. 7.
[12] Quoted by Cuénot, op. cit., p. 395.   [13] Ibid., p. 368.

ment of a feeling of oneness with the whole of mankind, something he had not previously experienced and which was to form an essential part of his evolutionary cosmology. It was also during this period that he experienced a vision of Christ, in which he saw the outlines of a painting of Christ merge into the rest of the world.[1]

In 1919 he returned to his scientific career and in 1920 became Professor of Geology at the Catholic Institute of Paris. 1923 saw him making his first visit to China, where he went on a palaeontological mission. Here in the vastness and isolation of Mongolia he saw that everything in the world could be described in terms of one single activity, and this gained expression in his *Mass on the World*, in which he, as God's priest, offered up to God ' on the altar of the entire earth, the travail and the suffering of the world '.[2]

On his return to France in 1924, he experienced his first clash with his superiors. He was forbidden to continue teaching because his ideas about original sin and its relation to evolution were considered unorthodox. After a period of unhappiness he returned to China in 1926, where he lived and worked for the best part of twenty years, with only occasional visits to Europe.

His next important work to be written was *Le Milieu Divin* in 1927. This he described as ' an essay on the interior life ', and in it he attempted to ' recapitulate the eternal lesson of the Church in the words of a man who, because he believes himself to feel deeply in tune with his own times, has sought to teach how to see God everywhere, to see him in all that is most hidden, most solid, and most ultimate in the world '.[3]

In 1938 he was appointed Director of the Laboratory of

[1] This is the first of ' Three stories in the style of Benson '. These stories are recounted in ' Christ in the World of Matter ', which forms one of the sections of *Hymn of the Universe*. They deal with the mystical experiences of a friend of Teilhard's, although it is generally recognized that they refer to Teilhard himself (*Hymn of the Universe*, p. 41). It is difficult to assess the importance of these incidents in the development of his world-view. Although it emphasizes the close relationship between Christ and matter, it does not feature as such in his thought.

[2] Quoted by C. Cuénot, *Teilhard de Chardin*, p. 50.

[3] *Le Milieu Divin*, p. 46.

B

Advanced Studies in Geology and Palaeontology in Paris, but his return to France was prevented by the outbreak of the Second World War. During the Japanese occupation of China his scientific work was considerably reduced, and it was at this period that his ideas reached their zenith. This was reflected in the production of *The Phenomenon of Man* in the late 1930's, with revisions of it during the first half of the 1940's.

Over-all however his many years in China were very productive ones in the sphere of his palaeontology. His best known contribution was his association with the finding and description of Sinanthropus (Peking Man), an important example of one form of early man. In addition to this he completed several important monographs on the late Cenozoic mammals of China, and played an invaluable part in the organization of Chinese palaeontological and geological research.

The attitude of his superiors to his views had not changed by the time of his return to France in 1946, and not only was he forbidden to publish or teach on philosophical subjects but he also had to refuse a very important Chair in the Collège de France.

In spite of these rebuffs he never once considered leaving the Society of Jesus for the greater freedom he could have enjoyed as a secular priest. He was convinced that to do this would be synonymous with cutting himself off from the will of God. To him the Society was his ' divine milieu ' and he accepted the restrictions imposed upon him with no outward sign of rebellion. However he did ensure that the necessary arrangements had been made for the publication of his writings after his death.[4]

Before moving to New York in 1951 he travelled widely, making many contacts in the scientific world including the formation of a deep friendship with Sir Julian Huxley.

In New York, until his death four years later, he worked at the Wenner-Gren Foundation where he was instrumental in the formulation of anthropological policy. His position also gave him opportunity to elaborate and disseminate his views on the future role of man in the universe.

[4] Cuénot, *op. cit.*, p. 307.

At the time of his death Teilhard's influence was limited to individuals, those who had been in his presence and who had been affected by his radiant personality, and by his stirring message of optimism and action.

It was with the publication, by an assorted group of sponsors, of *The Phenomenon of Man* (the French edition in 1955 and its English counterpart in 1959) that Teilhard burst upon the intellectual scene; and Teilhardism was born.

THE ESSENTIAL COMPONENTS OF HIS THOUGHT

The complexity of Teilhard's thought makes the task of summarizing it a difficult one. When it is also remembered that strands of his thought are found scattered throughout numerous essays and letters written over a period of many years, a summary must be seen for what it is — inadequate and perhaps even misleading.

In giving a brief résumé of his major work *The Phenomenon of Man*, we are on safer ground. While this work is by no means the complete expression of his thought, it does contain the essence of it. Furthermore, as it was written from a ' scientific ' point of view, it is of particular relevance for the scientist and for anyone interested in arriving at a scientifically-orientated view of the world.

Teilhard describes the book as a scientific treatise, which will examine man solely as a phenomenon. This however is not all, for it will consider the whole phenomenon of man. In spite of this, it is intended only as an introduction to an explanation of the world, an explanation in which man has been placed at the centre of the world.

Teilhard's dilemma is clearly stated at the outset. His thoughts as enshrined in *The Phenomenon of Man* are based on science, and yet at the same time his aim is to explain the *whole* phenomenon of man, and not simply isolated aspects of it. Metaphysics, theology and philosophy are not ingredients; science alone is put forward as the determining factor.

What Teilhard desires is a coherent explanation of the universe, one that will take everything into account. As a result, a materialist explanation of the world is inadequate because it recognizes only the external (or material) aspect of objects and persons at the expense of their inner aspect. In the same way a spiritual interpretation that concentrates solely on the inner (or spiritual) side of people and events is equally at fault. Put these two aspects together (the external and the internal), and a coherent explanation becomes possible.

The within and the without

There would be nothing remarkable in this if his concern was with an all-embracing approach to persons. Christianity has long been noted for exactly this emphasis. Teilhard however does not restrict his thinking to people. His insistence is not simply that people have a *within* (internal aspect) and a *without* (external aspect)), but that *matter as a whole* must be regarded in precisely these terms.

Working back from man and from man's experience of a within, Teilhard argues that, because man exhibits the phenomenon of *consciousness*, matter must also be viewed as possessing a form of consciousness. Consciousness, he claims, has a cosmic extension. The very stuff of the universe therefore has a double aspect to its structure; coextensive with a without, there is also a within.

According to Teilhard this is a phenomenal view, and for him a phenomenal view is *the* scientific point of view.

Although everything in the universe has a within and a without the development of the within with respect to the without varies. The within is best developed in man, the most complex entity in the universe, and in order to attempt to explain the relation between the within and the without, Teilhard postulated a basic law — the law of complexity and consciousness. According to this consciousness is best developed in the most complex and well-developed organisms, whereas in simple organisms it is rudimentary and poorly organized.

One further point of importance lies in Teilhard's use of the term ' energy '. In his striving after a coherent explanation of all things, and in his dislike of any fundamental dualism, he looked upon all energy as being psychic. He then subdivided it into tangential and radial energy, the former linking a particular element with similar elements, and the latter drawing any given element forwards.

Further principles

Teilhard's view of the world is an evolutionary one. Never-
theless it is permeated throughout with his own ideas, some
of which we have already met. Others appear when he is
dealing with the evolutionary process itself. For example,
the advent of life requires a long period of time, in order to
allow major changes to occur. Teilhard accepts this, but adds
a novel factor — a critical point. At this stage in the book
it is not clear what is the significance of a critical point. It is
described as ' an unparalleled moment on the curve of telluric
evolution '; it is the point of germination. From his use of
the term later on when discussing the birth of thought, its force
appears to lie in the uniqueness and never-to-be-repeated character of the particular event. He uses it to stress the importance
of the new form of being.

Teilhard's own approach to evolution again comes to the
fore when the expansion of life is under consideration. His
description of the main movements within evolutionary development is fairly orthodox, but he departs from the neo-
Darwinian explanation for the mechanism of evolution. For
Teilhard, the only complete form of heredity is provided by
orthogenesis, which is the name given to the belief that evolution has taken place in a straight line, towards a pre-set and
determined goal. In consequence, it has metaphysical overtones and is discounted as a scientific theory by most biologists.
In Teilhard's scheme of evolution it plays an indispensable
part in the ascent, rather than simply the spreading out, of life.

Having set forth his basic principles Teilhard is now in a
position to bring some of them together. He has claimed to
establish the existence of a within throughout the universe; and
also that evolution has a precise orientation and a privileged
axis. But with what is complexity supremely associated?
What structure is required for a highly-developed within?
Very simply, a nervous system. What stands out during
evolution is the differentiation of the nervous system. This
provides a direction, and therefore — according to Teilhard
— proves that evolution has a direction.

By a process of circular reasoning, the importance of the
nervous system confirms the importance of consciousness and
hence of the within throughout evolution. The impetus of the

world can now be explained in terms of some *inner* principle, and this becomes the guiding principle behind all evolutionary change. The development of new attributes during evolution is the result of the desires or of the temperament of the animal itself. The without of genetic changes is replaced by the within of innate desires. Here again Teilhard is out-of-line with present-day thinking on the subject; instead he has reverted to the Lamarckism of a former generation.

Teilhard's orthogenesis and Lamarckism are combined when he envisages evolution as one massive event — ' the grand orthogenesis of everything living towards a higher degree of immanent spontaneity '. He has rewritten the natural history of the world. It is ' nothing but an immense ramification of psychism seeking for itself through different forms '.

Noogenesis

At this point we may well ask what characterizes man? It can no longer be consciousness, as Teilhard has made this a feature of the whole universe. The answer lies in a highly-developed property of consciousness — reflection, which is the power acquired by a consciousness to turn in upon itself.

Man alone is capable of reflection. He no longer merely knows; he knows that he knows. However, before reflection could become a reality there had to be another critical point, the critical threshold of reflection. This he describes as ' an infinite leap forward ', a critical transformation, a mutation from zero to everything. By its very nature it had to be achieved at a single stroke. According to Teilhard this was a ' trans-experimental ' interval about which we can say nothing scientifically.

In the light of this admission we may find ourselves somewhat perplexed as to where his information comes from. We have however only to think of the principles he has already enunciated — pan-psychism (pan-consciousness), orthogenesis, critical points and the certainty of evolution. These provide the ' knowledge ', even though it is deductive rather than inductive. It is not scientifically acquired, but is a combination of arbitrary first principles.

The instantaneous leap from instinct to thought constitutes the process of *hominization*. Once thought has appeared on the scene it has to be developed, and it is this development of man's thinking powers that constitutes the process of noogenesis. The era of noogenesis is an entirely new era in evolution and as a result a new layer, the ' thinking layer ' is formed on the earth. The earth ' gets a new skin ', it finds its soul, the *noosphere* has come into existence.

In Teilhard's eyes these are the processes that have brought man as we now know him into existence. Not only therefore should they be of interest to modern man, they should drive him to action. He should realize his unique position as the arrow pointing the way to the final unification of the world. He is at the head of the whole movement of evolution, and he must accept the facts and face up to his cosmic responsibility. He must know that a suitable outcome to evolution is possible.

In saying these things however Teilhard is well aware that there are many to whom evolution is no more than an academic theory. They refuse to recognize that evolution is a general condition guiding the development of all spheres of human thought and action. They will not think in terms of biological space-time, and they are blind to the ' fact ' that the universe has been renewed by the discovery of the evolutionary idea. In other words they are not motivated by the potential dynamic of evolution.

To Teilhard such people are tragic examples of humanity. What is more they are dangerous because they refuse to recognize the only ' way out ' open to man. They refuse to serve the world because they do not believe in a future for the world. The hope of the world lies in its future, and its future depends upon men doing their utmost to forward their own evolution.

The importance of evolution for an understanding of the past is supreme, its importance for an understanding of our responsibilities in the present is crucial, and upon our response to these challenges will depend the whole of the future. Without evolution, Teilhard's vision would be non-existent.

The future — Omega

The arguments so far adduced by Teilhard provide him with an approach to the future. As evolution is an ascent towards consciousness, the future of the human race could be in one of two directions — either along a divergent or along a convergent path. A divergent path would lead to a state of diffusion of consciousnesses, and this Teilhard dismisses. By contrast, convergence must lead towards a definite point or state of integration. This is the direction Teilhard envisages, and the point where all consciousnesses will converge is termed the *Omega Point*.

This convergence of consciousnesses has an inevitable side-effect. Time and space are becoming humanized, or rather super-humanized. Consequently, the Universal and Personal are growing in the same direction and will culminate simultaneously in each other. Omega Point therefore is not only the Future-Universal but also the Hyper-Personal.

In other words, the universe is becoming more and more personalized. This conclusion is exceedingly important for Teilhard as a Christian, for it means that from an impersonal beginning the universe has acquired a personal meaning.

Omega Point is ' a distinct Centre radiating at the core of a system of centres '; ' it is a grouping in which personalisation of the All and personalisations of the elements reach their maximum, simultaneously and without merging '.

It lies in the future, but surprisingly it is also a present reality. Teilhard appears to reach this conclusion for negative reasons; were it only in the future, we would lack sufficient motivation to strive for survival of the human race during this present era.

From this conclusion it follows that not only is Omega the last term of its series, it is also outside all series. Although it emerges from the rise of consciousnesses, it has already emerged. Teilhard arrived at Omega through the humanization of time and space, but having reached it, he modifies his view — Omega, if it is to be Omega, must escape from the time and space that produced it.

But will Omega ever be reached? Will man destroy himself long before Omega Point is even in sight? Teilhard is essentially optimistic. Man is irreplaceable. Therefore he must reach the goal. The possibility of failure can never be entirely dismissed but failure would be equivalent to the universe committing abortion upon itself, and such a view is absurd.

Omega Point is indistinguishable, in part at least, from God, hence his use of the term ' God-Omega '. This is the end of the world, which itself is the critical point of maturation and escape. It may be achieved, and convergence will then take place in peace. Or it may be refused. This is the final ramification. Teilhard leaves us with this dilemma, although his whole trend is towards optimism and success rather than pessimism and failure.

This concludes the ' scientific ' section of *The Phenomenon of Man*. It is followed by a short epilogue on ' The Christian Phenomenon '. In this he links evolution and the general ascent of consciousnesses with the Lordship of Christ over these processes. God, the Centre of centres, coincides with the Omega Point of evolution. Hence, for the Christian, evolution is a magnificent means of enabling him to feel more at one with God. Christ is the centre of the converging world, and so Christogenesis is the extension of cosmogenesis and noogenesis. ' Christ invests himself organically with the very majesty of his creation '.

Cosmic, human and Christic

In the light of this summary of *The Phenomenon of Man* and of some of Teilhard's other writings, his thought can be said to consist of three main components, the cosmic, the human and the Christic, all three being part and parcel of one great whole — his synthesis of the universe. All three are of an evolutionary nature, and so his cosmos is in reality a cosmogenesis and his God ' a God of cosmogenesis, that is a God of evolution '.[1] By this he appears to mean that God is an integral part of the evolutionary process,[2] in the sense that God and the evolving universe are now united the one with the other. From this it follows that evolution has a Christic centre,[3] mankind's duty being to advance this Christification. Hence the third component, the human, links the cosmic and the Christic, constituting as it does the thinking layer (the noosphere) which in time lies between the living layer (the biosphere) and the ultra-human (Omega, Christ or God).

It can be seen that this view of the world would be distorted beyond recognition were any one of the three components to be

[1] C. Cuénot, *Teilhard de Chardin*, p. 369.   [2] *Ibid.*, p. 293.
[3] *Ibid.*, p. 272.

removed. Not only are they all essential to his vision, but they are reducible to each other, and deducible from each other. Before being able to construct such a system Teilhard had to postulate a number of more fundamental principles.

He himself regarded the relation between *the one and the many* as the central feature of his system.[4] This led him to search for an answer which would give unity to a world of diversity and plurality. A synthesis that would lend coherence both to the whole of the universe and to every part of it, from the atoms at one end to God at the other, had to be found.

Such a vision inevitably entailed a rejection of the dualism of mind and matter, and even of a rigid distinction between God and man. Instead he ranged himself with the monists, for whom the perception of multiplicity must be completed in some form of unity.[5]

I have already alluded to the way in which he virtually (if not entirely) equated God with the evolutionary process. This was no accidental outcome of his visionary theorizing. It was closely associated with his view of Christ as the *organic* centre of the cosmos, and Christ's body as being equivalent to the cosmos itself. To Cuénot, such a view takes on a Christian character because it is derived from the incarnation, when Christ became a part of the cosmos, and from the resurrection, when He assumed the role of mover of the cosmos.[6]

The final point essential to his synthesis derives from the changing character of evolution from man onwards. Prior to man's appearance it was *divergent*, resulting in the production of an ever-increasing number and variety of living forms. In the case of man, however, or in the case of the noosphere, to use Teilhard's expression, evolution is *convergent*. As man's progress is dependent upon his intelligence rather than upon his undergoing bodily adaptation, it is restricted in its anatomical diversification. Rather, due to the roundness of the earth, the opposite is happening, men being drawn closer together by their social and mental interaction upon each other. From this Teilhard argues, as we have already seen, that future evolution will continue to be convergent and will ultimately become involuted in an ultra-personal Centre — the Omega

---

[4] *Ibid.*, pp. 377, 378.   [5] *Ibid.*, p. 379.   [6] *Ibid.*, pp. 122-124.

Point. This will happen at the Parousia, the second coming of Christ, when the Omega Point, which is the centre of human convergence, will be seen to be one and the same as Christ the Omega.[7]

This, to Teilhard, is the perfect synthesis of science and Christianity, both of which are vindicated because they lend themselves to such a synthesis

[7] *Ibid.*, p. 294.

2 THE PROJECT

I. A PHENOMENOLOGY OF THE UNIVERSE

Man and the world can be studied from a number of different standpoints. It is possible to view them in philosophical, theological, metaphysical or scientific terms. Furthermore, each of these categories can be further subdivided, and so for example in the scientific realm man can be approached from a psychological, neurological, physiological, biochemical, cytological or sociological angle. Each of these is a legitimate field of study, and yet each is limited, making no attempt at framing a total view of man, let alone a total view of man within the universe.

In terms of these disciplines, an over-all view of the world can be obtained only by amalgamating them, an extremely difficult task today when they are all so specialized and restricted in outlook. In practice, of course, it is a task attempted by very few.

There is, however, another way of gaining a total view of man and the world, and this is by studying them purely as a phenomenon. This involves attempting to understand the universe as it is seen by an observer, and as it is seen in its totality rather than as the sum of its integral parts.

This was the enterprise undertaken by Teilhard, and in his hands it became a phenomenology of the cosmic. Such a phenomenology therefore is, according to Wildiers, ' a science which seeks to describe the universe as an observable phenomenon in its totality and its intrinsic cohesion, and to discover the meaning concealed in that totality '.[1]

[1] *An Introduction to Teilhard de Chardin*, p. 48.

From this it becomes clear that a phenomenology of this nature must, if it is to be valid, have a sound scientific substructure. But it is not, in the strict sense, a scientific cosmology. Although it is closely linked with science, and although it is a synthetic and regulatory unitary ideal of science,[2] it is not synonymous with science. This is necessitated by its basic aim, which is to provide a coherent explanation for the whole world phenomenon. The subsidiary sciences can go so far, after which only extrapolations and hypotheses are able to provide the inner meaning concealed within the phenomenon. It occupies therefore a middle position between the natural sciences on the one hand and philosophy proper on the other.[3]

A number of consequences follow from this. In the first place, a phenomenology of the cosmos is neither metaphysics proper, nor is it philosophy proper. This does not mean to say that it has no connection with these disciplines. It has very definite metaphysical and philosophical consequences, although in itself it resolves none of the ultimate questions regarding the cosmos and it says nothing about the purpose or meaning of this world and of man's existence in it.[4] Teilhard could not avoid introducing great theological and philosophical themes. More important, his phenomenology as a system provides a substructure with which theology and philosophy must reckon; they, in their turn, will have to be modified if his phenomenology is accepted as *the* most important criterion to which every world-view must conform.

Second, Teilhard's phenomenology seeks for a ' vision ' of the real. Basic to Teilhard's system is his attempt to ' see ', that is to say, ' to try to develop a homogeneous and coherent perspective of our general extended experience of man '.[5] To him, the world was a whole or a totality which unfolds, and which unfolds when subjected to intellectual and logical analysis. In other words, the secret of the phenomenon of man and the world can be discovered only at the level of thought and

[2] C. Cuénot, *Science and Faith in Teilhard de Chardin* (Garnstone Press, 1967), p. 66. This book is volume 2 in The Teilhard Study Library; volume 1 is *Evolution, Marxism and Christianity,* by various contributors.
[3] Wildiers, *op. cit.,* p. 49.   [4] *Ibid.,* p. 105.   [5] *PM,* p. 39.

rationality. Its achievements are to be judged at this level and at no other.

If we link up this idea with the need felt by Teilhard for a coherent synthesis of his Christianity and his science, we will have some idea of the major part played by the intellect in his world-view. Although his Christianity was largely separate from his phenomenology, his existential need was only satisfied in terms of the coincidence of the two. Apart from this rational phenomenology, therefore, he would have found himself in the midst of the modern dilemma. From this it follows that anyone unable to follow Teilhard to the limits of his phenomenology, on intellectual grounds, will if he is consistent find his existential synthesis of limited value.

Third, as Teilhard's phenomenology is based upon what he conceived to be the current position in science, it is (and will remain) open to being supplemented and improved.[6] It was not put forward as the final answer to the problems of the universe,[7] although as it is an all-embracing system of thought it is difficult for most people to treat it as anything other than final and complete. It must also be mentioned that if the scientific ideas upon which the phenomenology was built were to undergo radical alteration, Teilhard's phenomenology with all the hope enshrined in it for certain people would disappear with them.

Finally, how does this phenomenology work in practice and what type of thinking does it demand of its adherents? As everything is united in a single, coherent whole, all chance and contingence as well as all resistance and contradiction are eliminated. A single idea bringing together the most diverse orders of the real, the world and God must triumph. It must find a constant in the universe.[8] Consequently, as man is aware of a ' within ', or a ' psychic ', aspect to his make-up, this principle must be extended to apply to all other living things, and even to non-living matter. Such a principle is readily incorporated within a scientific phenomenology, not because it bears any relation to available scientific evidence, but because it must be accepted in order to arrive at a coherent

---

Wildiers, *op. cit.*, p. 50.   [7] *PM*, p. 318.
[8] E. Rideau, *Teilhard de Chardin : A Guide to his Thought*, p. 64.

account of the universe. Without some form of pan-psychism, unity would be lost and synthesis on a phenomenal plane would be impossible. It is sufficient for Teilhard to show that something is plausible. As long as he can do this, he can maintain a unitary scheme of things — at least to the satisfaction of certain individuals.

In the light of this analysis of Teilhard's phenomenology, it may be more accurate to say that the underlying principle behind his phenomenology is not science as such, but an *awareness of the physical* and of that which is observable in nature. This allows him to bring out what he believes is implicit in the real, without being limited by a rigid scientific methodology. In other words, he has adopted a completely different methodology — a sort of philosophy that unites theory and reality, in a highly personal way. Although it is essentially an intellectual approach to reality, it is the intellectual approach of one man, and as a result is highly coloured by the psychological demands of this one individual.

We may ask why facts must have an inner meaning or law of their being, on a plane superficial to that of ultimate meaning and yet deeper than that revealed by scientific investigation? We may also ask how, if such an inner meaning exists, it can be confidently revealed? It is one thing to learn that the purely external method of phenomenology can discover that which is interior,[9] but it is quite another thing to be convinced of this. One gains the impression that the driving force behind accepting such a principle is the degree of anguish and fear engendered in an individual by the discord and nihilism of the modern world.

II. THE NATURE OF HIS SCIENCE

Some hints have already been given as to the type of scientific thinking adopted by Teilhard in the formulation of his phenomenology of the universe. However, in view of the emphasis placed on science by Teilhard (for example he stressed that *The Phenomenon of Man* was to be viewed as science and nothing else) we must pursue this issue further.

[9] C. F. Mooney, *Teilhard de Chardin and the Mystery of Christ*, p. 38.

Although it has been suggested by one writer[1] that *The Phenomenon of Man* was described as science rather than theology in order to give it a chance of being passed by his religious superiors, this seems hardly likely and not at all in character with the whole tenor of Teilhard's life. There is no doubt that he meant it as science, and not as metaphysics, theology or philosophy. His subject was man, man *solely* as a phenomenon, but the *whole* phenomenon.[2]

The question is what he meant by science. Most of his critics have not paused to ask this question, but assuming his science to be the same as theirs have plunged headlong into their literary tirades. Hence the ruthless criticisms by such eminent scientists as Professor G. G. Simpson,[3] Sir Peter Medawar[4] and Sir Alistair Hardy,[5] and by the historian of science and evangelical, Professor R. Hooykaas.[6]

It is clear from what we may term his orthodox geological and palaeontological articles[7] that in his scientific work he rigorously applied the principles of careful observation and experimentation to check foregoing hypotheses, and to suggest possible useful avenues for future work. He was a modern scientist of a very high calibre.

Science in this sense can be termed ' analytical '. It approaches problems by reducing them to their simplest known constituents, and with increasing knowledge gradually building up a more satisfactory picture of the system concerned. This is the approach of modern science.

For Teilhard, however, this was science at its *elementary* level, a level which had to be outgrown to enable it to pass on to its far more *advanced* task of ' synthesis '.[8] Consequently, when analytical methods of investigation yielded no further

---

[1] F. H. Cleobury, ' God, creation and evolution ' in *The Modern Churchman, 10* (1966), p. 18.　　　　[2] *PM*, p. 31.

[3] *Scientific American, 202* (1960), pp. 201-207.

[4] *Mind, 70* (1961), pp. 99-106.　　　　[5] *The Living Stream.*

[6] *Free University Quarterly, 9* (1963), pp. 1-57 and 58-83.

[7] For example, many of the articles reprinted in *The Appearance of Man*. These essays, spanning the years 1913-1954, are mainly of a semi-popular nature and range in scope from the orthodox palaeontology of ' The prehistoric excavations of Peking ' to the largely speculative ' The singularities of the human species '.　　　　[8] *PM*, p. 312.
See also his *Science and Christ* (Collins, 1968), pp. 21-31.

information on a particular topic, he passed on to the 'synthetic' aspect of science, which ' is . . . led to foresee and place its stakes on the *future* and the *all* '.[9]

According to Teilhard science can, and science must, see things whole. If this is accepted, the most profitable way of seeing man, for instance, is not as a collection of cells, however much might be known about the cells themselves, nor as a system of interacting organs and tissues, nor as a social animal, nor as a mechanism capable of highly complex learning patterns, nor even as a combination of all four plus many other descriptions. Man must be seen in his relation to the whole of the universe, from the atoms at its beginning to its culmination when the synthesis and completion of all things in God-Omega will finalize evolution. Inevitably there is much in this which is not open to direct observation and experiment. Teilhard surmounts these ' trans-experimental ' obstacles by a mixture of analogy from the rest of science,[10] faith[11] and logic.[12]

We may conclude that the guiding principles of ' synthetic ' science would appear to be: belief in the pre-eminent significance of man in nature, and belief in the progress and ultimate success of evolution.

Hence when reduced to its essentials, ' synthetic ' science is nothing more than a reaffirmation of the underlying presuppositions of his science worked out in a logical manner. Unlike ' analytical ' science it adds no new information to the system. It merely elucidates what has been present from the start.

This should not surprise us, as a science capable only of suggesting *possible* explanations for *certain* phenomena within the universe would have little value for a synthesis embracing *all* events within that same universe. Teilhard's science was not so confined — it did indeed explain *all* phenomena, such that positive statements appear more in keeping with it than do hypotheses. Consequently, in his own words, ' neither in its impetus nor its achievements can science go to its limits without becoming tinged with mysticism and charged with faith '.[13] The science underlying his phenomenology, therefore, leans

9 *Idem.*   10 *Ibid.*, p. 61.   11 *Ibid.*, p. 311.
12 *Ibid.*, p. 68.   13 *Ibid.*, p. 311.

C

more heavily upon philosophical presuppositions and logic than upon the less pretentious method of observation and experiment. In such an approach he was not original. He was following in the steps of such people as Bergson, Lloyd Morgan and Smuts, who in their differing ways as emergent evolutionists strove to bring out the character, direction and significance of evolution.[14] Their religious and their evolutionary views were closely dependent upon each other.

The many apparent absurdities in Teilhard's works can now be seen in a new light. To say, for example, that inorganic matter has a 'within' and a form of consciousness is something about which empirical science can say nothing. But to a vitalist, as Teilhard was, it does have meaning. In order to arrive at this conclusion, Teilhard argued that although every mass is modified by its velocity, we do not see change in the mass. In other words, there is no absolute appearance of a new dimension. By analogy, therefore, consciousness recognized only in man is present in a veiled form throughout the cosmos.[15]

This example is typical of Teilhard's approach. Having started with *empirical* science, he abandons it in favour of *synthetic* science when it can take him no further.

When the senses can no longer help him, he resorts to logic and reason, *still in the name of science*. In his eyes this is science because it is still within the realm of material phenomena.

He is consistent then in claiming on the one hand that *The Phenomenon of Man* contains 'purely scientific reflections',[16] and on the other confessing that a conclusion he has come to is 'strictly undemonstrable to science'.[17] What is most unfortunate is that he uses the same word to signify different things. This interpretation is I think supported by O'Connell when he claims that the word 'mémoire', translated 'treatise' in the preface to *The Phenomenon of Man*, carries the suggestion that the scientist, when he reflects on the meaning of his ordinary practice of science, becomes aware that his approach has

---

[14] C. E. Raven, *Teilhard de Chardin : Scientist and Seer*, p. 145.
[15] *PM*, pp. 59-61.   [16] *Ibid.*, p. 31.   [17] *Ibid.*, p. 311.

been only a partial one.[18]

The question we should be asking ourselves is this: How useful is a vitalistic approach, such as the one Teilhard adopted, to the forwarding of empirical science? Bernard Towers looked upon Teilhard as a scientific pioneer and generalizer, who propounded ' truly creative hypotheses '.[19] Hypotheses are essential to scientific advance, but only those hypotheses which are open to rejection or verification. To say as Towers does that the ' law of increasing complexity-consciousness ' ' allows for the probability . . . of intelligent beings on other planets ' and that ' it has relevance to proven phenomena in the field of extrasensory perception '[20] is an example of making statements which are so general as to have little, if any, value. It is difficult to see how the majority of Teilhard's generalizations can, or ever will, be tested.

In fact it could be argued that Teilhard's approach removes the necessity, or even the relevance, of ' analytical ' science. The striking feature about his essays making up *The Appearance of Man* is that the speculative ones are based to only a limited extent upon actual scientific findings. This is to be expected, as a science which has already explained the universe leaves little room for further advance based upon observation. Although Teilhard allows his ' synthetic ' science to include a preliminary ' analytical ' aspect, in practice the need for analysis has disappeared.

To what then can we ascribe the attraction and power of his writings, when we bear in mind their influence on eminent scientists as well as on ordinary laymen?

The testimonies of the scientists concerned — including Sir Julian Huxley,[21] Dr Joseph Needham[22] and Dr W. H. Thorpe[23] — are revealing. Each of them holds an evolutionary worldview incorporating religious ideas — albeit in one case ' without revelation '. What distinguishes them from some of the

[18] R. J. O'Connell, ' Teilhard's scientific attitude ' in *Journal of the American Scientific Affiliation, 18* (1966), p. 80.

[19] ' Scientific master versus pioneer: Teilhard and Medawar ' in *The Listener*, 15 April 1965, pp. 557, 558.

[20] *Idem.*   [21] Introduction to *PM*, pp. 11-30.

[22] ' Cosmologist of the future ' in *New Statesman*, 7 November 1959, pp. 632, 633.   [23] *Science, Man and Morals.*

scientists who oppose Teilhard's position is that their religious or neo-religious views form an integral part of their evolution-istic system, which in turn forms the basis of their detailed thinking about the future of man and his universe.

To such people Teilhard's immense evolutionary thinking, with its great originality of expression when describing his vision of the future, is bound to prove stimulating and exciting. To them the details of his vision are not important, nor whether it incorporates scientific precision. For instance, to Thorpe ' much of his greatness lies in his ability to demon-strate . . . the existence, in regard to the animal kingdom, of an overall tendency towards increasing complexity and the de-velopment of mind '.[24]

To these men it is his vision which carries the day, and this is equally true in the case of the majority of his followers. He brought together science, philosophy and theology (as even Raven[25] and Le Morvan,[26] two ardent disciples, admit) in order to construct a vast picture of the world.

The essence of his vision is that the whole universe is of an evolutionary nature, and that it is absolutely necessary to adopt an evolutionary approach to nature. So convinced is he of this that he identifies a positive knowledge of things with the study of their development.[27] He is able to hold such a view because to him evolution is much more than a theory, ' it is a general condition to which all theories, all hypotheses, all systems must bow and which they must satisfy hence-forward if they are to be thinkable and true '.[28] Is it any wonder then that, for Teilhard, ' evolution is a light illumina-ting all facts, a curve that all lines must follow '?[29]

As if this were not sufficient, he proceeds to equate the recognition and spreading of evolutionary ideas with ' the most prodigious event, perhaps, ever recorded by history '.[30] It may be asked whether he considered it more important even than the incarnation of Christ.

---

[24] *Ibid.*, p. 56.   [25] *Op. cit.*, p. 206.
[26] M. E. R. Le Morvan, *Pierre Teilhard de Chardin* (Catholic Truth Society, no date), p. 15.   [27] *PM*, p. 51.   [28] *Ibid.*, p. 241.   [29] *Idem.*
[30] *Idem.* In *Science and Christ*, Teilhard describes Christianity as ' the very religion of evolution ' (p. 124), while evolution is regarded as ' the hand of God gathering us back to himself ' (p. 213).

In regarding evolution as something given rather than as something observed, Teilhard's philosophy is more idealistic than naturalistic.[31]. This comes out most clearly in the quotation given above from *The Phenomenon of Man*, where he states explicitly that, instead of being a theory, it is a general condition to which all theories and systems must conform. The impact of such a position is felt when the future of evolution is discussed. For Teilhard it *must* continue to a successful end; man *must* reach his goal. If his evolutionary scheme had been based upon observation, he could not have been sure.

Here is the problem posed by Teilhardism. A priest of the Roman Catholic church presents us with a thorough-going, all-inclusive, evolutionistic philosophy; a man to whom evolutionism is the central pivot of the universe.

In concluding this section, we might briefly compare the details of his evolutionary scheme with general evolutionary views today.

Characteristic of his evolutionism is its Lamarckism and orthogenesis, the scant attention paid to genetics and the presence of critical points.

Lamarckism is generally understood as the doctrine of acquired characters, although it also involves an orthogenetic development due to an upward urge within the organism concerned. Teilhard specifically repudiates a view of evolutionary change using natural selection as a mechanism, and replaces a Lamarckian explanation.[32] Whatever may be the status of natural selection as a mechanism, there is no convincing evidence in favour of, for example, a tiger ' handing on the soul of a carnivore ',[33] as Teilhard would like us to believe.

Following on from this Teilhard sees orthogenesis as the only complete form of heredity.[34] Orthogenesis in the sense of evolution along a straight and predetermined line has definite metaphysical overtones, and understandably is in disfavour with biologists. Teilhard claims not to use the word in this

---

[31] Cornelius Van Til, ' Pierre Teilhard de Chardin ' in *The Westminster Theological Journal, 28* (1966), p. 133.
[32] *PM*, p. 166.   [33] *Idem.*   [34] *Ibid.*, p. 120.

sense, but for the manner in which terms succeed each other in a historical sequence towards 'increasing degrees of centro-complexity '.[35]   If by this he means that everything has a direction of change, it explains nothing.   If on the other hand he means that everything has a *specific* direction of change towards Omega, he is virtually using the term in its classical sense.   In spite of his denial, his use of the term suggests he is endeavouring to signify a process directed from above, that is, from Omega — the motive power of cosmogenesis.

With respect to genetics, Teilhard thought this subject did not concern him directly, even in *The Phenomenon of Man*.[36] This is disconcerting as it strongly suggests that when refer-ring to the rates of evolutionary change he was influenced by factors more philosophical than scientific.   His vagueness about these rates of change, for example, when he mentions the 'almost explosive acceleration of noogenesis ' in one para-graph, and our 'almost imperceptible advance ' in the next,[37] confirms our fears.

His use of the concept of critical points is essential to his whole system.   The two most important points are those responsible for the birth of life[38] and for the birth of reflection.[39] At the first, the cell was born and at the second, thought.   It is the second which is the essential one for Teilhard, as he must find a radical difference between man and the rest of the animal kingdom, a difference which does not involve any anatomical discontinuity.   With genetics behind him, he imagined the birth of thought occurring at a single stroke, ' a mutation from zero to everything ',[40] one particular being lacking the ability to think and the next possessing it.

The ease with which he could postulate this emanated from the emphasis he placed upon the 'within' as opposed to the 'without' of organisms.   A critical point is a feature of the 'within', and may be accompanied by no discernible change in the 'without'.   The initiative lies with Teilhard's followers to demonstrate the value of this hypothesis for evolutionary thinking, as it corresponds to no demonstrable evidence.

Without penetrating any further into all aspects of his

---

[35] *Idem.*   [36] *Ibid.*, pp. 152, 153.   [37] *Ibid.*, p. 280.
[38] *Ibid.*, p. 112.   [39] *Ibid.*, p. 187.   [40] *Ibid.*, p. 190.

evolutionary scheme, we can see that it is more in line with philosophical evolutionism than with any genetically-orientated, mechanistic approach to evolution. We might expect even vitalists to take seriously that part of their whole which is empirical science. But it seems that in Teilhard's case this was not so.[41]

III. THE LAW OF COMPLEXITY-CONSCIOUSNESS

This law brings us to the heart of Teilhard's synthesis and of its dependence upon evolution. In addition it paves the way for his views regarding the future.

To Teilhard, within the process of biological evolution there could be discerned a general direction of movement — an intrinsic orientation — from the simple to the complex. For example, this process could be followed from the elementary particles to the atoms, from atoms to molecules, and so on to unicellular and multi-cellular living creatures, through the increasingly complex animals and ending ultimately in man. In other words, within cosmogenesis a key role is played by complexity.[1]

Recognizing Pascal's two infinities or ' abysses ' of the very small and the very great, Teilhard added a third: that of complexity.[2] Essentially this third infinite of the infinitely complex appears when the concept of cosmic time is taken into account. The importance of this idea is that it enabled Teilhard to see life as a specific effect of complexified matter, a property in itself co-extensive with the whole stuff of the cosmos, but perceptible to us only where complexity exceeds a certain critical value.[3] This, in turn, led on to his view of man as ' the one on whom and in whom the universe enfolds itself ';[4] he is in union with the world, no longer an alien in it but now its goal.

This movement towards increasing complexity is a movement towards increasingly intricate mechanisms and a greater

[41] For a discussion of Teilhard's evolutionary ideas, see B. Delfgaauw, *Evolution. The Theory of Teilhard de Chardin* (Collins, Fontana, 1969).
[1] *PM*, p. 329.
[2] Teilhard de Chardin, *Man's Place in Nature* (Collins, 1966), p. 23.
[3] *Ibid.*, p. 24.   [4] *Ibid.*, p. 36.

richness of internal organization and quality of concentration.[5] It is an objective fact on a purely scientific level.

This however is only one aspect of this law. Running parallel to this increasing complexity, evolution is characterized by another feature — increasing consciousness. We have already noted, within this view, the presence throughout the universe of a ' within ' in all levels of matter, and it is this ' within ' Teilhard is thinking of when the word ' consciousness ' is used. As he considered evolution, he recognized a gradual growth of psychic properties with a steady advance in the complexity of the nervous system, reaching its climax in man.

Of course, the two processes of increasing complexity and ascending psychism may be independent of one another, especially as psychism cannot be associated with any structural entity in plants and non-living matter. However, Teilhard and his followers consider that the parallelism between the two suggests that one is a consequence of the other.[6]

As I have already pointed out, the belief in the universal presence of some form of psychism throughout the world is a consequence, not of scientific investigation, but of Teilhard's phenomenology. There is no direct scientific evidence for the universal presence of psychism, which is defined by Teilhard as anything ' from the most rudimentary forms of interior perception imaginable to the human phenomenon of reflective thought '.[7] Can this aspect of the law, then, be scientific? Teilhard has no doubt that it is, but we should remember that for him anything that is an extension of physical reality is scientific, whether or not it has been demonstrated to exist by scientific techniques. We must also bear in mind the fact that for this law to have universal validity, psychism must also be universal, for if the law cannot be extended backwards to infinity in the past, neither can it be extended forwards to infinity in the future. Were this law to collapse, so would the whole of Teilhard's grand synthesis. As Wildiers has phrased it: ' it is this law that in his view affords us the key to a correct view of evolution — which in its turn is a central phenomenon, apart from which the universe cannot be integrated '.[8]

[5] N. M. Wildiers, *An Introduction to Teilhard de Chardin*, p. 73.
[6] *Ibid.*, p. 75.   [7] *PM*, p. 62.   [8] *Op. cit.*, p. 79.

Before we move on to the application of this law to the future, there is one further extension of it we might consider. This is that, in the case of man, ' spiritual perfection (or conscious " centreity ") and material synthesis (or complexity) are but the two aspects or connected parts of one and the same phenomenon '.[9] This enabled Teilhard to advance from the position that all things in the universe have a within as well as a without, to belief in the gradual dominance of the within in comparison to the without.[10] The end result of this process would be Omega — at which point the within would have vanquished the without, and so would consist solely of a collection of individual consciousnesses.

In a letter, Teilhard wrote: ' the past has revealed to me how the future is built '.[11] Indeed, as the years went by his interest in the past waned as his thoughts became centred more and more upon the future. What is important for us at this juncture is to understand the connection between the two. In the law of complexity-consciousness, Teilhard believed he had found a single evolutionary pattern up to the present, and so treating this as a scientific hypothesis he extrapolated it into the future. Hence, as evolution was seen by him as an ascent towards man and reflective consciousness, he concluded that it must continue to advance in the direction of increasing consciousness and increasing complexity. And so, at the apex of evolution Teilhard postulated a supreme consciousness, which would be the result of the convergence of the universe towards a supreme centre — the ultimate of all ultimates.

To Teilhard, this was a serious extrapolation,[12] having the validity of genuine scientific knowledge of the future. Its reliability is said to lie midway between the certainty of mathematics or astronomy and the confidence we can place in some guesses or conjectures.[13]

To what extent is this true? Is it a valid scientific postulate?

In the first place, its validity depends upon the validity of the law of complexity-consciousness. In addition to what has already been said on this, we can add that undoubtedly there

[9] *PM*, p. 66.   [10] *Idem.*   [11] *Letters from a Traveller*, p. 207.
[12] *The Appearance of Man*, p. 244.   [13] Wildiers, *op. cit.*, p. 90.

is a correlation between psychic quality and the arrangement of the nervous system. We can probably also go a step further and state that there is a correlation between psychic quality and complexity of the nervous system — at least, at a fairly gross level. This is a matter of scientific observation. However, this falls far short of the universal applicability of the law of complexity-consciousness. It cannot therefore be considered as a scientific law in the usual sense of the term, and so cannot be extrapolated into the future as a genuine scientific hypothesis.

Another serious question arises over the nature of past evolution as compared with possible future evolution. Teilhard treats evolution as one vast, continuous process. The cosmos and everything in it is, in reality, a cosmogenesis. Man is not a fortuitous or accidental phenomenon, but evolution's crowning success. He is the growing point of the universe; no, more, he is ' evolution become reflexively conscious of itself '.[14] In Teilhard's eyes, then, man will continue to forward the movement of evolution along the same path as before. Noogenesis is the continuation of biogenesis.

This vision assumes, however, that evolution will continue as before, now that it is psychosocial rather than biological, and also assumes that man will wish to forward his own evolution. There is no justification, in scientific terms, for equating psychosocial with biological evolution, and no justification for believing that it will continue as before. We are confronted with an entirely new process, operating on very different lines from past evolution, for the simple reason that whereas past evolution was genetically-based, any future evolution will be primarily non-genetic. For Teilhard, though, the concept of evolution is essentially in terms of his philosophical phenomenalism, rather than in terms of scientific evolutionism.

What emerges from a study of psychosocial evolution is that man is the agent solely responsible for it. This agrees closely with Teilhard's position, and in both systems of thought, man may fail. With Teilhard, however, the prospects of failure are much less, and should failure occur, the whole

---

[14] E. Rideau, *Teilhard de Chardin : A Guide to his Thought*, p. 53.

purpose of cosmogenesis would have been thwarted, and the religious purpose of life would be extinguished. The meaning of the two systems is, therefore, radically different.

IV. THE FUTURE

When we turn our attention to the future of the universe, we are moving into the realm of thought which was, for Teilhard, the major discovery of his life. Indeed, were his views on the future to be excised from his work, his whole picture of the world would be considerably mutilated and robbed of one of its essential elements.[1]

As we approach this subject, we need to bear in mind the fact that the future Teilhard considered was not the immediate future, but the whole future of the human race and of the world. His eyes were fixed, not on the next 100 years or so, but on the remaining n millions of years open to life on this planet. As in the rest of his phenomenology, he adopted the standpoint of the natural scientist, and not of the philosopher or the historian. His chief concern was with the future of man as a biological species in an evolving cosmic process. Themes such as over-population, world famine and nuclear destruction played only a very minor part in his outlook.

a. Unification

The one idea basic to all Teilhard's thinking concerning the future is that mankind — as a species — is being drawn together both externally and internally in an ever-increasing unification. Instead of the divergence characteristic of all past evolution, man is converging upon himself. He is being brought together physically, mentally and spiritually. He is becoming one.

Wherever Teilhard looked, he found confirmation for this view. Whether in research, or technology, or atomic power, he could see hope for mankind because he could see super-creativeness,[2] humanity cerebralizing itself,[3] and the growing convergence and concentration of mankind.[4]

---

[1] N. M. Wildiers, *An Introduction to Teilhard de Chardin*, p. 84.
[2] *The Future of Man*, p. 146.   [3] *Ibid.*, p. 173.   [4] *Ibid.*, p. 153.

The unification of mankind is an essential prerequisite for mankind's continued convergence in the future. It is a further stage in the unfolding of the law of complexity-consciousness, and it is also put forward as a factual statement of what is happening to us, and around us, at the moment.

It is legitimate for us to ask, therefore, whether his intense optimism is justified. Do we see developing around us a common endeavour in the fields of science, thought, art, ethics and religion? Do we find in these realms a concentration of energies and resources as have never existed before?[5] Do we observe in the thoughts and feelings of men a process of fermentation at work, pointing toward greater unification?[6]

It must be admitted that Teilhard's optimism was not of a naïve kind; it was fed by love of the world and by his concentration upon the distant, rather than the immediate, future. His optimism is of the tense, almost painful kind, buoyed up by a hope that defies present appearances.[7] He did also confess that, for the present, the cosmic machine appears to have ' gone into reverse '.[8] He was able to explain these present difficulties by introducing the idea of a growth-crisis,[9] a ' critical crossing of the Equator ' by the wave of hominization.[10]

What are we to say about his optimism? Clearly, it was something he derived not simply from his phenomenology. It was an act of faith on his part, and was closely connected with his Christian faith. In other words, it went beyond even his concept of the scientific, and so it is alarming to find, at an early stage in his scientific phenomenology of the future, a distinctively religious element. This is important because he claimed that his phenomenology, both of the past and the future, was derived solely from a study of the phenomenon of the world. The introduction of a religious element into his view of unification strongly suggests that his view of the future owes far less to purely scientific theorizing than he ever admitted. There is a powerful existential and arbitrary ele-

[5] Wildiers, op. cit., p. 96.
[6] Ibid., pp. 95, 96.
[7] H. Blocher, Interchange, 1 (1967), p. 17.
[8] PM, p. 282.
[9] Blocher, op. cit., p. 17.
[10] Man's Place in Nature, pp. 102, 103.

ment in it, and this is something we should never forget.
His optimism can also be ascribed to his comparative neglect of the present. His interest lay so much in the end of
history, and he was so certain of the triumph of unanimity,
that he was inclined to neglect present human oppression and
degradation.[11]

An additional factor to account for his optimism was his
bias towards the universal and the general at the expense of the
individual and the personal. Perhaps due to his concentration on the physical, he repeatedly emphasized the primacy of
communities and of the whole. Consequently, any general
trend always assumed greater significance for him than the
price which may have to be paid by individuals for the fulfilment of this trend. He was therefore not sufficiently aware
of the poignancy, tragedy and utter despair of much human
misery in today's world. And so, although he repeatedly used
the phrase ' union differentiates ', it never went beyond the
expression of an empirical statement,[12] and it never took on
any meaning for the world of living reality.

b. Socialization

This is the next stage forwards for man, as a species, after
unification. As its name suggests, it is a specific coming
together of mankind into increasingly compact societies. It
continues the process away from the individual, and herein
lies one of the dangers implicit in Teilhard's system. Will it
result in more and more depersonalization of man?

His adherents tend to argue that socialization will have the
opposite effect, because of the potentiality within real community for creating diversity.[13] This however does nothing
more than take us back to Teilhard's optimism, while it bears
little resemblance to the evidence afforded by the totalitarian
régimes of recent times. In fact, Teilhard's reaction to these
régimes affords us salutary evidence as to the idealistic nature
of the socialization he envisaged. Teilhard's espousal, in
general outline, of Fascism shows the type of path his system
could take if put into practice. For example, in 1937 he could

---

[11] E. Rideau, *Teilhard de Chardin : A Guide to his Thought*, p. 123.
[12] *Ibid.*, p. 115.   [13] Wildiers, *op. cit.*, p. 97.

write: 'Fascism quite possibly represents a pretty successful blueprint for the world of tomorrow. . . . Fascism opens its arms to the future. . . . Its ambition is to embrace vast wholes in its empire'.[14] Although he condemned what he described as the 'most ghastly fetters'[15] of Communism and National-Socialism, and although he did not condone the materialism of totalitarian mystiques,[16] yet he never seemed to have a sufficiently high regard, in practice, for the freedom of human personality.

c. Planetization

This is Teilhard's intermediate state between socialization, with its tenuous link with the present, and the ultimate unity — Omega. It is the cosmic organizing process aimed at global solidarity. It is the state of the earth when human consciousness is reaching, but has not yet arrived at, the climax of its evolution. It is the process whereby consciousness is super-centrating 'itself in the bosom of a Mankind totally reflexive upon itself'.[17] Ultimately, planetization 'by interiorising itself under the influence of the Sense of Evolution, can physically have but one effect: it can only personalise us more and more, and eventually . . . divinise us through access to some Supreme Centre of universal convergence'.[18]

The stage is now set for mankind's convergence into Omega.

d. Omega

When confronted by Omega we find ourselves in the sphere of the hyper-personal; we are 'beyond the collective'.[19]

Teilhard arrived at point Omega by imagining that in the heart of 'a universe prolonged along its axis of complexity, there exists a divine centre of convergence'.[20] But what is Omega? It is, or will be, 'the autonomous centre of all centres',[21] it is a kind of super-organism, it is a suprapersonal

---

[14] Rideau, op. cit., p. 478. This is a quotation from Sauvons l'humanité, 1937, in Science et Christ, pp. 181, 182, some of Teilhard's writings. Also, Science and Christ, pp. 140, 141. [15] PM, p. 282.
[16] Rideau, op. cit., p. 479. [17] The Future of Man, p. 133.
[18] Ibid., pp. 135, 136. [19] PM, pp. 279ff.
[20] The Future of Man, p. 122. [21] PM, p. 297.

unity, it is ' a distinct Centre radiating at the core of a system of centres '.[22] More specifically, it possesses the attributes of autonomy, actuality, irreversibility and transcendence.[23] What is very important to realize is that it has no connection with matter. By the time it is reached, the ' within ' is the whole of existence, the ' without ' having been completely displaced. This is brought out by Teilhard in a dramatic description of the formation of Omega. He writes: ' is it not conceivable that Mankind, at the end of its totalisation . . . may reach a critical level of maturity where, leaving Earth and stars . . . it will detach itself from this planet and join the one true, irreversible essence of things, the Omega point? . . . a simple metamorphosis and arrival at the supreme synthesis. An escape from the planet, not in space or outwardly, but spiritually and inwardly '.[24]

It is difficult to be sure how much further than this Teilhard went on the phenomenological plane. This far we have seen that he applied the term ' Omega ' to a state of collective re-flection at the end of the evolutionary process. Undoubtedly it had, for him, personal overtones. On one occasion, within the main phenomenal section of *The Phenomenon of Man*, he used the term ' God-Omega ';[25] and he concluded the work by saying that he had had to make all things double back upon ' someone '.[26] His main emphasis upon Omega was as a personal Being, as Christ, and as this was derived from speci-fically Christian thinking, this theme will be developed further in the next section.

We are however left with two relevant issues to discuss at this point.

First, Teilhard accepted Nietzsche's view that man is made to be surpassed.[27] Although there are differences between their theories of the future, Nietzsche looking for-ward to a superman and Teilhard to a super-mankind,[28] in both cases man as we know him is inadequate. The goal of the future lies beyond man and even beyond matter; it lies

22 *Ibid.*, p. 288.   23 *Ibid.*, p. 297.
24 *The Future of Man*, pp. 122, 123.
25 *PM*, p. 316.   26 *Ibid.*, p. 318.
27 L. Paul, *Alternatives to Christian Belief* (Doubleday, 1967), p. 32.
28 Wildiers, *op. cit.*, p. 101.

in the formation of a super-organism, comprising a collection of consciousnesses. In other words, it lies beyond the biological. ' His noosphere contains a vast apparatus, continually growing and cross-fertilizing, of *objectified* intellect and spirit from which the biological `draws sustenance and even *raison d'etre* '.[29] Although we are still on the phenomenal plane, one essential part of the phenomenon has completely disappeared. The tables have been turned upside-down, and from a scientific view-point, we are left not with science but with anti-science. That which we are now able to observe throughout the universe, and which is the basis of reality — matter — has gone. It has been replaced by that which is observable only within a very limited part of the universe — consciousness. What is more, wherever consciousness is at present obvious, it is always dependent on the biological. To reverse this scheme of things may satisfy a philosophical longing, but it is hard to justify in terms of a scientific phenomenology.

To use Leslie Paul's terse phrase, ' the noosphere negates the biosphere '[30] in Teilhard's thinking. What is more, this revolution introduces a fatal inconsistency into his phenomenology. In order to achieve unity and coherence in his thinking, Teilhard had to posit the existence of consciousness in all forms of matter within the universe. This was in accordance with his dictum that everything within the universe must be present in some primordial form.[31] If this is the case at the beginning of the universe, it is difficult to understand why, logically, it should not apply equally forcefully to the end of the universe. As this principle of unity is basic to his phenomenological scheme, his failure to apply it to the future invalidates the whole of his scheme.

Second, we may wonder why there must be an end to man and to the universe. Is a process of convergence inevitable? Is there any reason why increasing complexity and increasing consciousness should not continue in parallel, rather than in convergent, directions? Why, indeed, should there be an ultimate of any description?

The justification for introducing convergence into an ac-

[29] Paul, *op. cit.,* p. 35.   [30] *Idem.*   [31] *Cf. PM,* p. 64.

count of the future is the convergence seen now in the case of man. This convergence is essentially a physical and geographical one; the mental convergence advocated by Teilhard is of a more questionable nature. Can a convergence of the 'without' be extrapolated forwards as a convergence of the 'within'? What reliance can be placed upon the continuous nature of what is essentially a discontinuous process? Apart from this objection, there is still another discontinuity to be faced. The divergence of evolution up to man is replaced, once man is reached, by a convergence. The alteration in this fundamental aspect of the evolutionary process is a difficult principle to be accommodated within a phenomenal scheme based on the principle of coherence and unity. It is a problem ignored by Teilhard.

In the light of these difficulties, how did Teilhard find a place in his phenomenal scheme for the principle of convergence? The answer is simple: he went beyond the limitations of phenomenology and resorted to Christian ideas. One passage he wrote demonstrates this admirably. 'In affirming the existence of this supreme convergence, we are going beyond the evidence of pure experience, for observation of our daily setbacks would suggest that its realization must be postponed so indefinitely into the future as to be quite unattainable. It is only the Christian dogma of the mystical body, faith in a spiritual organism . . . that can assign a real term to our journey towards "catholicity".'[32]

This brings us to the Christian phenomenon within Teilhard's thought.

V. CHRISTOLOGY

A convenient place to commence a consideration of Teilhard's Christology is with the necessity of the Christian faith in forwarding and eventually bringing to fruition the evolutionary process.

On a purely phenomenal plane Teilhard was able to put forward a hypothesis regarding the *probability* of convergence. In order to go further than this, to a hypothesis of *actual* con-

---

[32] Rideau, *op. cit.*, pp. 566, 567. This is a quotation from *La crise présente*, 1937, in *Cahiers Pierre Teilhard de Chardin*, No. 3, p. 95.

D

vergence,[1] information of a different order was required. What was essential for his existential synthesis was the ability to be able to state categorically that we are actually converging towards a supreme centre. He had to be sure that an opening existed, and this was possible only by way of an act of faith based on rational grounds.[2] At this point, ' faith ' is faith in the world's future, as opposed to specific Christian faith;[3] it is however a step away from phenomenology and towards a Christian synthesis.

Not only must we know that convergence is actually taking place now, we must also be assured of the success of evolution. We must know, not simply that something is at the peak of evolution, but that Someone is there.[4] Without this knowledge, man will see no purpose in striving to forward evolution. A universal love is the only way in which we are able to love,[5] and it is the driving force necessary to inspire and draw man on.

What emerges from this is that Teilhard viewed Omega in two distinct ways. On the one hand it was the end product of natural evolution. This, he discovered, did not satisfy him. As he says: ' I made my way to Omega Point through the cosmos and biology, but it was still at arm's length '.[6] It was still a finite entity, and could not logically be identical with the Christ-God.[7] More was required, and so on the other hand, there was the *real* Omega.[8] This Omega is Christ or God; it is already in existence and is ' loving and lovable at this very moment '.[9] The *real* Omega is independent of natural forces; it is the last term of the series, but is also outside all series; it escapes from space and time.[10] In other words, it is Teilhard's conception of the Christian God.

In Omega therefore, Teilhard finds something which is ' not only a potential centre, but something real, something which makes irreversible, something self-sufficient, capable of bear-

[1] C. F. Mooney, *Teilhard de Chardin and the Mystery of Christ*, pp. 47, 48.   [2] *PM*, p. 257.   [3] Mooney, *op. cit.*, p. 48.
[4] *The Future of Man*, p. 279.   [5] *PM*, p. 293.
[6] E. Rideau, *Teilhard de Chardin : A Guide to his Thought*, pp. 160, 161. Quoted from *Le coeur de la matière*, unpublished, 1930, p. 21.
[7] Rideau, *ibid.*, p. 181.   [8] Mooney, *op. cit.*, p. 54.
[9] *Idem.*   [10] *PM*, p. 297.

ing the weight of a world in evolution, of acting as a keystone of the universe '.[11] What Teilhard has been compelled to do is to assert the primacy of being over becoming for the final stage of evolution.[12] Teilhard's two conceptions of Omega obviously present us with considerable difficulties. Was he referring to one entity or to two? Alternatively, did he view Omega as one entity with different appearances, dependent on the route by which it was approached, that is, through nature or through Christian revelation? Or a third alternative may be: did he use the two conceptions in an interchangeable manner? Without any question there is ambiguity on this issue. Whereas on some occasions Omega seems to possess the attributes of divinity, that is, personality, presentness, transcendence, unity, distinctness; on others it is ' partially actual ', ' partially transcendent ' and of ' maximum complexity '.[13] It has been claimed that ' Omega becomes Christ only by an act of faith ',[14] with the corollary that Omega only ' reveals itself to the man who is prepared to encounter it as the person of Christ the Redeemer '.[15]

There can be no doubt that Omega must be both the end result of a natural process, and the God or Christ of Christianity. He had thus achieved in Omega the perfect synthesis of science and Christianity, so essential to his inner life. But did he succeed? Did he manage to rid his thinking of the compartmentalization he so abhorred?

Undoubtedly, he was largely successful at all levels below Omega, within the framework of his concept of science and of his version of Christianity. He succeeded in holding together his science and his Christianity in a remarkable synthesis. One cannot fail to be impressed by the magnificence and scope of his vision. He loved the world and he loved Christ; as a consequence, he was able to worship Christ in every aspect of the world around him. He could pray with absolute sincerity: ' over every living thing which is to spring up, to grow, to

[11] C. Cuénot, *Science and Faith in Teilhard de Chardin*, p. 70.
[12] Mooney, *op. cit.*, p. 56.   [13] Rideau, *op. cit.*, p. 150.
[14] F. G. Elliott, ' The Christology of Pierre Teilhard de Chardin ' in *Evolution, Marxism and Christianity* (Garnstone Press, 1967) p. 97.
[15] *Ibid.*, p. 98.

flower, to ripen during this day say again the words: This is my Body. And over every death-force which waits in readiness to corrode, to wither, to cut down, speak again your commanding words which express the supreme mystery of faith: This is my Blood.'[16]

For him cosmogenesis was Christogenesis, while the church (that is, the Roman Catholic church) was the agent responsible for Christogenesis. Through evolution, a body fit for Christ was being prepared, while matter itself was being Christified. These ideas give some insight into the dichotomy within his thought, largely implicit in these statements, but which would become explicit when confronted by the problem of Omega.

What are we to make of his Christology?

First, at Omega, he is forced to revert to the *dualism* he fought so much to avoid. He is forced to appeal to the God of revelation for certainty regarding the outcome of evolution. He is back at the old categories of science and faith.

This dualism becomes obvious when we consider two of the characteristics of Omega. In the first place, although it is ' the last term of its series, it is also outside all series ';[17] second, while it emerges from the rise of consciousnesses, it has already emerged.[18]

These two characteristics are most significant because, as we shall see shortly, they mean that Teilhard's God fits in with orthodox beliefs — in a general way at least, whereas his premises do not permit such a conclusion to be drawn. If he had remained faithful to his premises, he would have arrived at a natural god, complete only at the end of the universal process. At the present time such a god would be incomplete — a pre-god perhaps.[19] He rejects this conclusion, and has been forced to accept a dualistic solution to his problem, having previously rejected the premise of dualism.

In spite of this conclusion, it is difficult to see how Teilhard's God can be an absolute person, as he has worked up to God from below. Such a God, therefore, must be relative with respect to the consciousnesses from which he has emerged.

And what of Teilhard's Christ? How could God, who will

---

[16] *The Mass on the World*, p. 23.   [17] *PM*, p. 297.   [18] *Idem*.
[19] J. Macquarrie, ' The natural theology of Teilhard de Chardin ' in *The Expository Times*, 72 (1961), p. 337.

be completed only at point Omega, have become incarnate as real God in human flesh? Can Christ have been truly God when God the Father was not truly God? In asking such questions we are pushing Teilhard's system to a logical conclusion, on the assumption that it was a consistent and monistic system. However, as we have already seen, he avoided such issues by reverting to dualistic thinking when it came to a Christian interpretation of point Omega.

Sir Julian Huxley found Teilhard's thought on point Omega not fully clear.[20] The matter is a crucial one for Teilhard's whole phenomenal system. On his own criteria it stands or falls on its coherency.[21] We are faced with two alternatives. If we accept his system as a fully coherent one it amounts to no more than evolutionary naturalism. If we allow his introduction of a transcendent God, his system as a system has little value. It is internally self-contradictory, and all that remains of it are a number of instances of evocative terminology.

In spite of this considerable difficulty, Teilhard's synthesis — inadequate as it is in the end — still worked for Teilhard, and does so today for many people. Why? Probably because it invites people to make a common, organized effort for man's development.[22] This, in turn, is more closely related to a quality of inward experience than to any external and objective criteria.[23] It is those in need of intellectual and spiritual deliverance from the conflicts of the modern world, and who are drawn towards some form of spiritual solution to the problem, who are likely to be instinctively drawn towards Teilhard. In the end, it is the mystical element in Teilhard's synthesis that triumphs over the rational, and it is the mystical side of Teilhardism which remains as the determinative factor in a person's approach to it.

His orthodox conclusion does mean he escapes from the pantheist camp, as his God is more than the fusion of the centres resulting from the ultimate convergence of the universe.[24] In addition, he took great care to make clear that together with the concentration of creatures within God-

---

[20] Introduction to *PM*, p. 19.
[21] *PM*, pp. 58, 268. [22] Rideau, *op. cit.*, p. 24.
[23] N. M. Wildiers, *An Introduction to Teilhard de Chardin*, p. 33.
[24] *PM*, p. 338.

Omega, there was also a differentiation between them.[25] From his conclusions therefore the charge of pantheism cannot be levelled against him.

Teilhard's dualism at Omega is important for another reason. It enabled him to remain an orthodox Roman Catholic. As Cuénot remarks: ' the theological and biblical bases of this spirituality are therefore more than reassuring. It would be easy to demonstrate that Teilhard is directly in the Jesuit tradition of the *Spiritual Exercises* of St. Ignatius Loyola, and exercises himself to see God present and acting in all things, in all beings '.[26] Or again, Elliot sees his Christology as being fundamentally in agreement with the living faith of the church, while, in his opinion, few others harmonize so well with the whole of the Holy Scripture.[27]

What is implied by these testimonies is that Teilhard retained the fundamental conceptions of Catholic doctrine — the transcendence of God, creation, spirit, evil; the parousia; the church, the Virgin Mary, *etc.* This does not mean, however, that he viewed them in traditional terms. This he certainly did not do. Instead he transposed them from the framework of a static view of the world into the dimensions of a world in cosmogenesis. Neither does it mean that he placed equal emphasis upon each of them — quite clearly, he emphasized the cosmic role of Christ far more than His redemptive role. It is also questionable whether his cosmogenic interpretations of the doctrines contained within them the *essence* of their meaning under the traditional system. For example, can the literal, physical return of Christ be equated, in any meaningful sense, with the convergence of all consciousnesses into the Supreme Consciousness at Omega? Furthermore, is there any biblical teaching to suggest that Christ's return will coincide with the moment at which mankind will have attained its natural completion?[28]

Following on from this, there is one other point we might note in passing. This is the major and essential part played

[25] *Le Milieu Divin*, p. 116.
[26] *Science and Faith in Teilhard de Chardin*, p. 24.
[27] *Op. cit.*, p. 87. However, in the last paper he wrote Teilhard pleaded for ' a new theology ', see *Science and Christ*, p. 220.
[28] Wildiers, *op. cit.*, p. 141.

by evolution in every aspect of Teilhard's thought. This is such an obvious point that it could easily be neglected. Every doctrine has been radically altered by being viewed through evolutionary spectacles. As a result, Teilhard could say that 'the great mystery of Christianity is not exactly the appearance, but the transparence, of God in the universe'.[29] This is a fundamental shift in outlook, from traditional transcendence-language to the immanental perspective of his Christology.[30] Instead of the universe witnessing to the character of God, it now demonstrates God through what it actually is. In the light of this, it is not surprising to learn that the role of the Christian and the church is to foster evolution. The links between evolution and Christ are so close that as evolution is advanced the process of Christification is correspondingly advanced. In short, 'evolution · subsumes the whole purpose of creation, incarnation and redemption'.[31]

Before leaving the question of Teilhard's Christology, the place of *mysticism* in his world-view should be mentioned.

The great conflict of Teilhard's inner life was to resolve the problem of how the man who believes in heaven and the cross can continue to believe seriously in the value of worldly occupations.[32] He was faced with the classical dilemma of the radical dualism of matter and spirit, of body and soul.

As has already been pointed out, for Teilhard this was not simply an intellectual difficulty; for him it had profound personal implications, and the answer he arrived at met his deepest mystical aspirations as well as providing the background to his thinking.

His solution lay in seeing the universe, and everything in it, as comprising a single whole.[33] Hence he substituted a monistic approach to reality for a dualistic one. This let him postulate on the one hand that Christ can and should transform matter, and on the other that we approach Christ through matter.

As a result he can say, in the first place, that the function of the Christian ' is to divinise the world in Jesus Christ ',[34] and in the second, that the arms and the heart which God opens

[29] *Le Milieu Divin*, p. 131.
[30] A. O. Dyson, 'Marxism, evolution and the person of Christ' in *Evolution, Marxism and Christianity*, p. 81.   [31] *Ibid.*, p. 82.
[32] *Le Milieu Divin*, p. 51.   [33] *Ibid.*, p. 61.   [34] *Ibid.*, p. 72.

to him ' are nothing less than all the united powers of the world which, penetrated and permeated to their depths by your will . . . converge upon my being to . . . bear it along towards the centre of your fire '.[35]

This centre where all the elements of the universe meet is for him the ' divine milieu '.[36] Consequently, for Teilhard the world became the body of Christ,[37] this being just one aspect of the union which he saw between God, the transcendent personal, and the universe in evolution.[38]

This is the heart of Teilhard's mysticism, the origins of which are probably to be found in the sacramentalism of the Roman Catholic church. What Teilhard did was to increase yet further the physical aspect of dogma, incorporating this simultaneously into an evolutionary philosophical scheme.

Teilhard's mysticism is of exceptional importance because it highlights fundamental aspects of his science.

It explains why he was content to confine himself in his science to phenomena. As man's power to explain nature increases, so his knowledge of God increases. Furthermore, as man increases his control over nature, man himself becomes greater, creation as a whole becomes more beautiful, the more perfect is adoration and the more Christ finds a body worthy of resurrection.[39]

The evolution of the cosmos, that is cosmogenesis, is the Christification of all things as everything is moving towards the supreme personal centre, which is Omega or God. Teilhard's mysticism ensures that science is essential for God to be disclosed.

To go a step further, in such a system there can be no place for, or need of, any specifically theological or philosophical concepts. This of course does not mean that such ideas are not present in his writings as undisclosed presuppositions. What it does mean is that he recognized no necessity to discuss such issues. A by-product of this procedure is that almost any theological interpretation can be accommodated by one of his phenomenal principles. For example, the origin of man can be explained theologically in ' special creation ' or ' evolu-

[35] *Ibid.*, p. 126.   [36] *Ibid.*, p. 114.   [37] *Ibid.*, p. 155.
[38] Quoted by C. Cuénot, *Teilhard de Chardin*, p. 293.
[39] *Ibid.*, p. 123.

tionary' terms; either can fit equally well into his principle of
the 'infinite leap forward'.[40]

VI. FURTHER ASPECTS OF HIS THEOLOGY

In addition to what has already been mentioned regarding
Teilhard's theology, a number of further points need stressing.
In the first place, his theology was in the tradition of Duns
Scotus' incarnational theology. Christ is held to be the goal
and crowning-point not only of the supernatural but of the
natural order.[1] From the beginning, the whole creation was
planned with the God-man in view. Even if man had not
fallen, the Word would have become man. The incarnation
was in the original plan of creation, and Christ is the master-
piece of God's creation.[2] While this viewpoint allowed Teilhard to bring together his science and his Christian faith in
the cosmic Christ, he did this at the expense of Christ's purpose
as redeemer. The redemption has become largely lost in the
incarnation, especially as he sees the cross primarily as the
supreme means used by Christ to urge the world on towards
its term.[3]

The central problem of Teilhardism is the relation of the
One and the Many. Evil and sin are simply by-products of
evolution. They are peripheral deviations of a natural process, having nothing to do with the central problem of life.
It is often objected that it is not valid to criticize Teilhard for
this, as his concern was with working out a phenomenology
and not a theology. This, however, is an over-simplification.
Teilhard's phenomenology is the ultimate criterion for the
remainder of his thinking, including his theology, which was
radically modified in consequence.

To him, then, evil is a by-product of evolution. This is because evolution advances by means of groping and chance,
with the result that checks and mistakes are always possible.
Furthermore, for every one success in evolution there are
many failures.[4]

---

[40] *PM*, pp. 187, 188.
[1] N. M. Wildiers, *An Introduction to Teilhard de Chardin*, p. 131.
[2] *Ibid.*, pp. 131, 132.
[3] E. Rideau, *Teilhard de Chardin : A Guide to his Thought*, p. 225.
[4] *PM*, pp. 339-341.

Kopp has expressed his position admirably: ' . . . if we see the universe as being in a state of becoming, imperfections must obviously be a part of the process, since anything arranging itself must necessarily include some disorder at every stage. Thus evil is structural stress of evolutionary creation. It counts for nothing in itself '.[5]

In speaking of suffering, Teilhard remarked that ' sufferers . . . are merely those who pay the price of universal progress and triumph '.[6] This is inevitable, if evil is viewed as a by-product of a dynamic and progressive movement. This too is his view of death; it ' is the regular, indispensable condition of the replacement of one individual by another along a phyletic stem '.[7] Why? Because it is ' the essential lever in the mechanism and upsurge of life '.[8]

The reason for Teilhard's sparce treatment of evil stems from his interest in the positive, rather than the negative, side of evolution.[9] In part, this may be due to the way in which in his own life he seems to have been so taken up with the love of God that little place was left for considerations of sin. However, his references to sin as ' a weakening or deviation caused by our personal faults ', or to bad actions as being ' positive gestures of disunion '[10] are most disquieting. Even if it may be argued that in these quotes he was not speaking theologically, we are left wondering what can be the value of any system, whatever its nature, which regards sin within a purely human framework.

The logical outcome of making evil a part of the evolutionary process is that, as scientific knowledge increases, evil decreases. The consequence of this is that when scientific knowledge will have reached its maximal point, evil will have been obliterated. And this is what Teilhard envisages when he describes the final convergence into Omega as taking place in peace.[11] However, as with his view of Omega, he is not always consistent, and there are occasions when he suggests that

---

[5] J. V. Kopp, *Teilhard de Chardin Explained* (The Mercier Press, 1964), p. 65.

[6] ' The meaning and constructive value of suffering ' in N. Braybrooke (editor), *Teilhard de Chardin : Pilgrim of the Future*, p. 25.

[7] *PM*, p. 340.   [8] *Idem.*   [9] *Ibid.,* p. 339.

[10] *Le Milieu Divin*, p. 80.   [11] *PM*, p. 316.

evil will increase rather than decrease.

His over-all picture of sin and evil is devoid of any connection with God and His holiness, or with the way in which this is expressed in the laws and commands He has given to men. But this is not surprising when we recall that in Teilhard's eyes juridical symbols sufficed only for society prior to the dawn of the modern, scientific-industrial stage.[12]

Furthermore, Teilhard makes no definite distinction between evil and sin. The Bible, however, never identifies sin with evil in general, as though it was nothing more than an attribute of imperfection. Its character is personal, moral and juridical. It is transgression of God's sovereign command, and is accompanied by guilt.[13]   With Teilhard, however, there is no sign of responsibility for sin, because he regards it as part and parcel of a natural process and not as a disruptive intrusion within the process. For him, the Fall is essentially a symbol of the world's incompleteness,[14] and not a historical event separating man from God.

In Teilhard's eyes, history is a homogeneous and continuous development: or, to use Blocher's description of his position, it is a ' one-act play, called Evolution-Creation-Incarnation-Redemption '.[15]   By contrast, the Bible views history as discontinuous, due to the entry of sin at the Fall, and so is divided into distinct phases: Creation—the Fall—Redemption. The incarnation in itself does not save; it is the means whereby atonement for sin can be made by Christ's death on the cross. Whereas the incarnation solves Teilhard's problem of the One and the Many, it is helpless, by itself, to deal with sin and with the problem of our reconciliation to God. Constantly, the biblical message is that we must be reconciled to God through the life, death and resurrection of Christ. We are dependent upon His grace and His initiative, to open our eyes and to reveal to us our own sinfulness and the only way to true life through Jesus Christ. Nowhere does Scripture ' invite us to make ourselves, our vision of phenomena, our mystic intuition the starting-point '.[16]

[12] Quoted by C. Cuénot, *Teilhard de Chardin*, p. 194.
[13] H. Blocher, ' The mystic vision of Teilhard de Chardin: a French Protestant view ' in *Interchange, 1* (1967), p. 78.
[14] *Idem.*   [15] *Idem.*   [16] *Ibid.*, p. 82.

A consequence of Teilhard's views on sin and evil is his position regarding salvation. Here again, the meaning of salvation is inextricably bound up with his evolutionism.

In his vision of the future, he pictures only two alternatives — either absolute optimism or absolute pessimism. Between these two extremes there is no middle way, ' because by its very nature progress is all or nothing '.[17] And so, either all men will finally converge into Omega, or none will. Hence he has dispensed with the necessity, or even relevance, of individual redemption. This is brought out in a different way in his discussion on ' hell ' at the end of Le Milieu Divin, in which he attempts to reconcile his own belief in the virtual impossibility of any man ever having been damned, with the official Roman Catholic belief in the reality of hell.[18]

This position has two consequences. In the first place the incarnation of Christ has only a universal evolutionary significance, with no meaning for individuals as individuals. In the second place salvation is made dependent upon the efforts of mankind as a whole, efforts to complete the mystical body of Christ. This explains the emphasis Teilhard laid upon the socialization of mankind, directed towards preventing the waste of human potential and with the object of speeding up the supreme development of mankind. This led him, and has since led his followers, into their dialogue with Marxists, whom they respect because of their concern for the social conditions of men and with whom they wish to find common ground. This is essential for Teilhardists as human socialization is man's hope of achieving the ultra-human condition necessary before Omega can be achieved.[19]

Finally, reference must be made to one way in which Teilhard is represented as being fully in line with at least some scriptural teaching. This concerns the similarity of his thought to certain of the views of Paul, and to a lesser extent, of John. It is Raven who reminds us that ' Teilhard in his whole Christian vision of the process of Cosmogenesis and Christification is . . . restating for us the theology of St. Paul as this came to its fullest expression '.[20]

---

[17] PM, p. 256. [18] Pp. 147-149. [19] Cf. Cuénot, op. cit., p. 235.
[20] C. E. Raven, Teilhard de Chardin : Scientist and Seer, p. 159.

By this he means that Paul, in his three last epistles, Philippians, Colossians and Ephesians, presents a vision of Christ as the consummator of all things in whom the whole universe finds its integration and fulfilment.

It is true that on a number of occasions throughout *Le Milieu Divin* Teilhard alludes to those words of Paul dealing with the extent and power of Christ's influence, and there is little doubt he was deeply moved by these ideas.

The most important one for Teilhard is that ' God shall be in all ',[21] which he probably took from Colossians 3: 11, where it is stated that ' Christ is all, and in all '. This he links with the anticipation of a unity of all things in an all-embracing personality, the Christ that is to be, based on Ephesians 4: 13 which looks forward to our coming ' to the unity of the faith and of the knowledge of the Son of God, to mature manhood, to the measure of the stature of the fulness of Christ '.

These ideas provide Teilhard with his vision of the cosmic Christ, the Christ who is the organic centre of the universe and the motive power of evolution. The statement ' Christ is in all' signifies to Teilhard that the resurrected body of Christ is coextensive with the cosmos.[22] Further, as evolution progresses mankind is moving towards a Christian community. In short, ' Christ is become cosmic, the cosmos is being Christified '.[23] This is the result of integrating the two visions of a mystic, universal Christ and a cosmic goal for evolution.

It is a pity that, in order to obtain such an organismic synthesis, Teilhard has lost the spiritual Christ. Unfortunately, he was concerned with only one aspect of Paul's thought, the one which appeared to coincide with ideas previously reached by rational means. His similarity to Paul is non-existent. Even their universal Christs are totally dissimilar. For the one Christ delivers individuals from sin and its consequences, uniting them one to another and to Christ as their Head. For the other Christ's function is to advance the noospheric evolution of mankind.

This difference reflects the more fundamental difference in their starting-points. For Paul this was God and His reve-

---

21 *PM,* p. 322.
22 Cuénot, *op. cit.,* p. 122.   23 Raven, *op. cit.,* p. 173.

lation; for Teilhard it was man and his awareness of the role he has to play in advancing his self-evolution.[24]

VII. DIALOGUE WITH MARXISTS

This subject is important, not simply because of the prominence given to the Teilhardian dialogue with Marxists by Teilhard's followers, but because of those features of Teilhard's synthesis it highlights.

The followers of Teilhard have in common with Marxists a faith in man, and the belief that man has a future. To quote Teilhard: ' by faith in man, we mean the more or less active and passionate conviction that mankind, taken in its organic and organized totality, has a future before it; a future formed not only of the succession of years, but of higher states to be reached by way of conquest '.[1]

To Teilhard, man *is* the meaning of the world, and this means that man must be conscious of his mission to conduct, and bring to completion, the evolution of the world.[2] Teilhard, then, does not seek to turn people away from the material world and from human effort. He magnifies and exalts them by integrating them in his synthesis.[3]

Although there are considerable differences of outlook between Teilhardians and Marxists on a number of issues — for example, for a Marxist the meaning of life and history is not a fact of *nature*, but a fact of *culture*[4] — they are united in their confidence in man and his ability to give to life and history a glorious meaning.[5]

For Teilhard's part, this confidence in man has been achieved only at great cost, namely the rejection of everything

---

[24] *Cf.* J. J. D. De Wit, 'Evolution as a Christocentrically directed process in Teilhard de Chardin ' in *Christian Perspectives 1962*, p. 53; also, ' Pierre Teilhard de Chardin ' in P. E. Hughes (editor), *Creative Minds in Contemporary Theology* (Eerdmans, 1966), pp. 407-450.

[1] Quoted by R. Garaudy, ' The meaning of life and history in Marx and Teilhard de Chardin: Teilhard's contribution to the dialogue between Christians and Marxists ' in *Evolution, Marxism and Christianity*, p. 59.

[2] Garaudy, *ibid.*, p. 65.   [3] *Ibid.*, p. 61.
[4] *Ibid.*, p. 68.   [5] *Ibid.*, p. 69.

tainted with world-denying elements.[6] This necessitated a revolution in his picture of God. Indeed, he started not with the doctrine of God, but with the person of Christ.[7] This led him to the position where he could talk properly about God only ' in terms of Christ as immanent and operative within the known cosmos '.[8] It is, then, only in terms of ' a physical, more organic form of Christology '[9] that there can be any *rapprochement* between Christians and Marxists. Anything suggestive of individual redemption, over against the redemptive consummation of the whole world, and anything suggestive of an unchanging God who is in some sense over against the processes of this present world can find no place in Teilhard's theology.

[6] A. O. Dyson, ' Marxism, evolution and the person of Christ ' in *Evolution, Marxism and Christianity*, p. 77.
[7] *Ibid.*, pp. 78, 79.   [8] *Ibid.*, p. 79.   [9] Quoted by Dyson, *idem.*

3 AN APPRAISAL

Although one may disagree with many aspects of Teilhard's thought, it has to be accepted that here was a man who took both the modern world and his Christian faith seriously. ' His concern was to blaze a trail for the new type of Christian of his dreams — one in whom love for the task of living here on earth in an evolving world would coincide with a love for Christ '.[1] His commitment to the modern world is of great value. It reminds us that the world is God's ' very good ' creation, which we are to master and subdue. We have no justification for despising it. Furthermore, according to the Bible, the cosmos bears witness to the Creator. We are reminded of this as we read Teilhard, although the details differ; he demonstrates that behind the universe there can be only God or absurdity, and to him only God makes sense. Finally, his abhorrence of a compartmentalized life is something to be greatly admired. Although I do not think he succeeded in proving his point, it is an effort to be improved upon rather than discarded.

Different aspects of his thought have affinities to such diverse people as Duns Scotus, the medieval scholastic, the philosophers Alexander and Whitehead, to Lloyd Morgan, an emergent evolutionist and to Huxley, an evolutionary humanist. What Teilhard did present to the world was twofold — a synthesis of a form of evolutionism and a form of mystical Christianity, together with the personal testimony of a very remarkable and very devout man, a mystic and a scientist.

The mysticism he presented overrode both empirical science

[1] N. M. Wildiers, *An Introduction to Teilhard de Chardin*, p. 161.

and biblical Christianity. While giving the appearance of being a prophet for the mid-twentieth century, he rejected the science of today and the biblical faith relevant for today and clung instead to the science and philosophy of the Greek heritage.

Whatever may have been Teilhard's own aims, it is difficult to avoid the conclusion that what stands out most clearly in his synthesis is his naturalism at the expense of his supernaturalism; man at the expense of God; and the world at the expense of Christ (in spite of his professions to love Christ more than anything else). Herein lies the danger of Teilhardism. Its emphasis on the incarnational and cosmic Christ, to the detriment of the redeeming Christ, can only lead to worship of a generalized nature-deity with consequent neglect of the transcendent triune God revealed in the Scriptures.

In gaining a cosmic Christ Teilhard lost the Christ of the Scriptures. Having based his world-view on man and the world, this was inevitable. From this it should not be concluded that no contact is possible between the Christ of the Scriptures and the world in which we live. On the contrary, we can go so far as to say that as we isolate Jesus Christ, the incarnate Son of God, from His world, we limit our vision of His glory and majesty, and we fail to worship Him as the all-powerful Creator and ever-present Upholder of this present world. With our hope founded in this Christ, and not in an organismic entity, it is our duty to present Him in the totality of His person and in terms of the whole of life.

Our starting-point however must be God and not man. God's revelation of Himself, of His activity in this world and of man's dependence upon Him, as shown to us in the Bible, is essential. It is the framework around which a comprehensive knowledge of the world can be built. Similarly, the creatorial and redemptive activities of Christ form an integral part of a total view of the world. These are biblical concepts which, for the Christian, should be fundamental principles.

Such biblical ideas are not stumbling-blocks in the way of effective communication in a scientific age. Rather, they constitute the dynamic elements of the Christian gospel, for without them all that would remain would be the shifting sands of existential relativism. Without them, we are back at Teil-

E

hard with his optimistic, but uncertain, hope in the face of an uncertain future. With them, we have the certainty of a faithful God and a sure Redeemer, and the challenge of a vast world around us.

THE WAY FORWARD

As we study Teilhard we are confronted on all sides by ultimate questions. What is the purpose of the world in general, and of our own existences in particular? What is the place of Christ in a vast, expanding universe? What is the final goal of the world, and of all the consciousnesses within it? For him, these were essential questions, to which satisfying answers had to be found, for his existence as a meaningful being was at stake. Consequently, any critical analysis of the framework of meaning which he elaborated must be accompanied by an alternative framework if it is to pave the way for a positive, world-affirming philosophy. What must be found, therefore, is a set of values which is seen to have reality and meaning in terms of the real world in which we live, that is, the world of nature, of biology, of personality, and also the world of hope, of longing, and of achievement.

In order to arrive at such a set of values, we will have to reach the conclusion that the world of our senses and our experience is a real world. What this means is that the world — including our own existences — is something which merits serious attention, and which will provide us with an intellectual and moral dynamic. This, of course, was the overriding aim of Teilhard's life. It is also the great aim of the world's religions and of serious humanists.

The problem is: Where does one begin? What is the starting-point?

For evolutionary humanists and for Teilhard, the starting-point is man, or, more precisely, man in the setting of his evolutionary upbringing. Although Teilhard strayed outside these terms of reference, the deciding factor in many of his views was man as an integral part of nature. Their starting-point then is an entity within the realm of nature. But is it a comprehensive description of that entity? Is man *only* a representative of the natural world? What is their justification for beginning with man?

The use of man as the starting-point is not self-evident. Although man is of cardinal importance in the world as we know it, this does not justify making him the final criterion of the world, especially against the background of an impersonal, mechanistic, evolutionary philosophy. Man as the central pivot and irresistible focal point of the universe is not a fact of nature. This is a presupposition based upon belief in man and in his powers to dominate nature and himself.

What is more, such an interpretation of man is no guarantee that the world will take on meaning and purpose. An autonomous man in an autonomous world can achieve greatness only if he is correctly programmed. But how can we be sure about his programming? The world of our senses provides little hope in this direction. If there is any knowledge to be obtained on this count, it must come from some source other than man. It must come from outside the realm of nature, and yet because it refers to man it will have direct relevance to the real world.

In other words, there is no certainty that an explanation of the world starting from man himself — as an entity within the real world — will provide a viable hope for life. Indeed, a philosophy confined to objects within the world of sense-data may well end as a world-denying, rather than a world-affirming, philosophy. It is at this point that Teilhard scores over many humanists. Unlike so many of them, he did not confine himself to the human condition, but ranged far and wide in a broad Christology. Where he failed was in his inconsistency over basic principles and not in the scope of his thought.

It is my contention that man can only be known, as a whole and in his relation to the universe, by approaching him from ' outside '. This in no way denies the validity of the many ways in which man can be investigated from the ' inside '. In very many areas this is the only method of approach available. For example, the structure of the brain or the liver, the functioning of the thyroid gland, the treatment of coronary thromboses, the development of awareness in the child, all these and many other factors in man's make-up can be investigated only by the activities of man himself. They are ' inside ' activities and as such reveal their secrets when treated as relatively isolated entities, and when suitably manipulated by man. This is due to the fact that man can look on them in a *fairly* objective way; he can remove a lobe from a liver (either from a human being or another mammal) and he can study it in numerous different ways. If he is rigorously scientific in his study, his own views and prejudices will not influence his findings too greatly. But, even here, it should be borne in mind that if he intends examining its fine structure, he will first have to ' fix ' and stain the (dead) tissue; in other words, he will have altered its ' real ' appearance. At the present time there is no alternative to this, and for practical purposes it does not appear to matter very much. However, it does remove by one step the certainty we can have about the structure of the ' real ' world, in terms of our own observations.

When we turn our attention to problems more intimately connected with man's perceptions, this uncertainty increases enormously and may reach the proportions of logical indeterminacy. MacKay[1] has considered the problem of what would be the consequences if, at some time in the future, a super-scientist could know from the outside what is going on in a man's brain and could calculate what is about to happen. Would this mean that the super-scientist would know the ' real truth ' about a decision before the man made it? Would this convert all his decisions into mere illusions? The dilemma arises over the fact that if the observer writes down a description of a future decision, the very act of believing this on the part of the man concerned would alter the decision itself. The decision would become out of date, and could not be the ' real truth ' in any universally binding sense. For the man concerned, it is logically indeterminate.[2] Although, in this illustration, the part played by the observer is larger than in most scientific situations, the principle underlined here is a general one.

The limitations to the extent of man's ' inside ' knowledge about himself are not due to inadequacy in present scientific

[1] D. M. MacKay, ' Man as a mechanism ' in D. M. MacKay (editor), *Christianity in a Mechanistic Universe* (Inter-Varsity Press, 1965), pp. 62-66.   [2] *Ibid.*, p. 64.

knowledge, but to the nature of the knowledge itself. Man is limited by his own involvement in the world. Whereas it is possible for him to escape to a large extent from individual systems, that is, from a *part* of his world, it is not possible for him to escape from the *whole* of his world. He is bound by his existence as man.

How then can man be known from ' outside '? Where can the appropriate knowledge be found? Is it possible to say how man is programmed as man, in any ultimate and meaningful way?

I believe this is possible in one way only, which is by viewing man in relation to the One who stands over against him — the One responsible for his existence as man. What is involved is a shift in ultimate responsibility from man as autonomous man to man-under-God. No movement away from the real world is implied. Rather, it is an attempt to view man in a larger, more appropriate setting.

In such a scheme the ultimate is God. What this means is that there is a real, viable, ultimate entity, existing apart from man and yet related to man by virtue of man's dependence upon it (or, as we shall see in Christian terms, upon *Him*). We are referring therefore to something definite, which as a result has to be taken into account in all descriptions of man and in all discussions concerned with the possibility of meaning and purpose in man's life. The term ' god ' is more than an *idea* or *word,* a function of man's religious instincts, and of descriptive value in analysing the psychological needs of certain individuals. On the contrary, God is the One who exists, He is ' The God Who is There ',[3] or, in different terminology, ' the final environment of what is there is God Himself, the one who has created everything else '.[4] It is of vital importance therefore that we understand the relationship between man and God, for no aspect of man's life is exempt from the influence of God. No part of man's life can be fully described without taking God into account; no area of human activity can possibly be exempt from the relevance of God.

[3] Title of a book by Francis A. Schaeffer (Hodder and Stoughton, 1968).
[4] *Ibid.,* p. 145.

But how can God be known and from where does the ' outside ' information about man come? In other words, how can man himself know what is God's view of man, and what are God's purposes for him? The orthodox Christian view is that God has taken the initiative, and has revealed Himself to man. Throughout the ages, God showed Himself in various ways and to differing degrees to certain individuals and groups of people. Accordingly, man's information about God gradually increased, until at a particular point in history the ultimate in cosmic unity was achieved — God became one with man in human terms. Jesus Christ, the God-man, the man whose very essence and nature demonstrated the activity of God, lived on this earth. Or, to express it in a different way — Jesus Christ, the Son of God, the second person in the Trinity, lived on this earth as a man but without the defects of other men. He was the most profound expression possible of the character and attributes of God; He revealed God in an absolute way, and He was (and still is) the only way to God.

In Jesus Christ, therefore, the most profound longings and aspirations of men can be satisfied. The unity of all knowledge stems from His person. The cosmos can never be completely alienated from Him, the destiny of individuals is determined by their reaction to Him, and personal fulfilment in a God-centred universe is found only in a life orientated with respect to His life, teachings and example.

Our argument so far has been that ' outside ' information about the condition of man comes from God, while information about God comes supremely through Jesus Christ. Interesting as these concepts are, it must be admitted they are rather nebulous. In themselves they are of little value in rescuing us from the morass of relativism and existentialism. Without more concrete pointers they leave us at the level of feeling and intuition, however religiously-inspired these may be. What is needed is definite information concerning the content of God's revelation to man, and concerning the actual claims, manner of life and pronouncements of Jesus Christ. The Christian position is that such relevant information is to be found in the Bible, which is the Word of God.

The Bible ' presents itself as God's communication of propositional truth, written in verbalized form, to those who are made in God's image '.[5] It is thus an objective expression of what God would have us know about man and his world, and about Himself. Unacceptable as this belief is to modern man, it derives its rationale from the character of God, and in terms of His character it is an eminently reasonable concept. Only when the existence of God, or at least His ability to act independently of man, is questioned *ab initio*, does it become unreasonable. This however brings us back to the nature of our assumptions regarding man and God.

With the Bible as the source of our knowledge on the nature and destiny of man, we can proceed to formulate the basic principles of his existence in the universe. Man and the world were created by a personal-infinite God, to whom man owes his existence and upon whom his world is dependent. From this God he can never completely escape, and to Him he is accountable. Furthermore, the world is a real world, as God has created it outside of Himself.[6] It is objectively real, and within it man has a vital role to play. Yet again, man was fashioned in the image of God, which can be seen in his capacity for spiritual, rational and moral activities. Although these have been obscured by man's rebellion against God they are still evident.

It is the greatness and the lostness of man which together constitute the supreme dialectic of the Bible. Having been created with the intention of exalting his Creator, the infinite God, man still has the potential of vast achievement. Herein lies the wonder of his intellectual ability, his capacity at formulating grand concepts, his ingenuity at plumbing the depths of nature, his colossal insight into his own condition and his relation to the world. But herein also lies his arrogant disdain of his Creator, his futile attempts at building his own universe, his dark loneliness in an empty void and the meaninglessness of an open-ended road to nowhere.

He is great and he is lost. This is the message of the Bible, but it is not the end. Unlike modern man, the Bible does not

[5] Francis A. Schaeffer, *Escape from Reason* (Inter-Varsity Press, 1968), p. 89.
[6] *Ibid.*, p. 86.

leave man at the edge of despair. It does not tell him he is a useless offshoot of a pointless world. While it tells him in no uncertain terms that he is lost because he is separated from God, it also directs him back to God through the person of Jesus Christ. Reconciliation with God is possible through a man — Jesus Christ. Spiritual harmony for the individual comes through participation in the world — in the person of Jesus Christ. There is no dichotomy here between the spiritual and the material; there is no escape from the real world. True fulfilment proceeds from a transformation of the individual. This in turn results from his reconciliation to God, which is made possible by the life, death and resurrection of Jesus Christ.

While this solution does not begin with man, it always keeps man in view. In this sense it is man-centred, although it has a God-centred dynamic. It is worldly, in the sense that it is carried out in space-time dimensions. It is realistic, because it views man as he is — real man in a real environment, and not idealized man in a mystical future.

The despair so characteristic of modern man, and in which Teilhard de Chardin had a part, is a result of a fundamental shift in thinking away from the transcendent God and towards man. The undue emphasis placed upon man has, paradoxically, highlighted his own inadequacy in an impersonal universe. Although Teilhard appears to have realized this, he was still affected by it because his Christian synthesis was based to a large extent upon man as an animal species rather than upon man in his relation to God. As long as a final solution to man's problems is made dependent upon the answers man himself is able to supply, despair will remain and hope will continue to be a mere illusion.